FISHING FOR GOD

—and vice versa

BY BILL ROONEY

PRESS

www.xulonpress.com

Table of Contents

Introduction

The sport and science of fishing have been at the core of who I am since that still-remembered day at about age six when Dad took me to a New Jersey lake and showed me the ropes (we anglers know them as "lines"). As I matured, however, I sensed that there is more to this pastime than catching fish: In the special places to which I was drawn by my piscatorial passion, I kept catching glimpses of greater goals, deeper meanings, richer reasons to live my life in certain ways that I could make out only dimly.

Helping to sharpen the picture were the aging process, my Christian faith, and certainly the influence of my wife Rita (as I write this we are celebrating our fifty-first year of marriage) and our four offspring, Karen, Kevin, Brian, and Kristin, and their spouses and young ones.

Still, nagging questions remained: Why, in a variety of special spots—on a wild trout stream in the Blue Ridge, or casting a surf rod into the huge, molten sun boiling up over the brink of the Atlantic, or sitting in an old rowboat with my best friend in the calm of an Ontario lake—why do I feel so ... utterly peaceful? So apart and yet so much a part of everything that's important in life? So totally . . . *loved*?

It is said that the Irish can be a wee bit light in the belfry at times. Guilty as charged. But it has come to me in my dotage that fishing can be a form of love. And where there is love, there is—you guessed it—God. God has graced me with the priceless gift of a pastime that reveals Himself to me, and in the process makes me want to reflect Him in our society. And—revelation of revelations—there's no doubt in my mind that even as I have "fished" for Him all my life, He has in turn set His hook into my soul and has been reeling me home to Him all that while. Wow!

A few words about what's between the covers here: With the exception of the very last piece, every article is nonfiction—these things actually happened. Most were written by me over the course of my forty-five-year career as a magazine editor and freelance writer. And most were published in the magazines I worked for or in outlets ranging from *Sports Afield* to the *Washington Post* to the in-flight airline magazines. Many of the shorter pieces herein appeared not long ago in our local newspaper, the Lexington (VA) *News-Gazette*. Quite a few involve our family, notably our two older grandboys, now-teenagers Grayson and Devin. The single article in Chapter 4, "Setting the Hook," describes a profound experience that dramatically changed our family's lives and is the main reason this book was written. And finally, at the end is "The Road to Tinkhamtown" by Corey Ford, a fictional account by a fine wordsmith that poignantly portrays how we humans are drawn to the natural world as God made it.

Because these stories were conceived over a period of probably forty years, and are not arranged chronologically, readers may experience a sort of where-am-I-and-when sensation. I know I felt it as I was trying to fit all these pieces together into a coherent whole. Bear with me—I'm getting old.

Thankfully, Rita and I are not yet too crotchety to dote on two delightful little bundles of "bait" lowered by the Master Fisherman—about two years ago as this is written, and just a couple of weeks apart—into the lives of our two youngest: son Brian and his wife Melissa, and daughter Kristin and husband Steve Davidson. One is named Sophia and the other Daniel. Certainly He has a plan for each of these little creatures and their parents. That plan, it is already apparent, will be built around love—the kind that requires no response, no payback. I can feel it every time I gather one of those bait-babies in my arms and walk around singing "Danny Boy" to him or her (the lyrics change to "Sophie Girl" as conditions require). I've always loved that old song, which expresses the sadness and love of an Irish father in a long-forgotten time as he watches his only son walk across the moors to go to war.

And so, as Rita and I move through our mid-seventies, God reels us in, slowly but inexorably, lifting us from the depths toward the Light. We're a bit long in the tooth to leap free of the surface anymore, like a smallmouth bass with a rocket in its tail, but occasionally we wallow on top like an old buster and get glimpses of what's in store for us.

Dedication

My Dad, Bill Rooney Sr., was the gentlest, most caring man I've ever known. He wasn't much of a fisherman, but on a fateful day of my sixth year seven decades ago, he ignited a spark that smolders in me to this day. Thanks, Dad.

Rita, the woman who has tolerated my passions and peccadillos for fifty-one years, is the catch of my life. She herself never succumbed to the lure of fishing, but that's just as well: she might have thrown me back! Love you, Reet.

Fr. Chuck Gallagher was a Jesuit priest, a consummate angler (though I doubt he ever wielded a rod), and certainly one of the best of God's gillnetters. Reet and I spent only one weekend under his tutelage, but he knew just the right bait, hooked us firmly, and reeled us to the Master Angler's waiting net. Godspeed, Chuck.

And so it began....

Almost seventy years ago, my father took me to a lake in central New Jersey and showed me how to thread a worm on a small hook, fix a bobber four or five feet up the line, and cast the works out under a bridge with an ancient metal rod and reel. After what seemed an hour but was probably ten minutes, the bobber started to jiggle, concentric rings rippling out from it as if to help rivet my attention.

"Dad! Dad! I think I have a bite!" I whispered (whispering just seemed right under these circumstances).

"Let him take it, Billy," Dad said, leaning back on his elbows on the grassy bank, the smoke from his pipe curling slowly into the bright sunlight.

"Dad—I can't see the bobber anymore!" The little bit of white cork had suddenly plunged into the depths, and I was well beyond whispering.

"Let him have it, son," Dad said. "He needs to chew on that worm awhile and get the hook into his mouth." How could he stay so calm?

I still remember those exquisitely unbearable moments. And I remember the crushing disappointment when the bobber rose to the surface and I reeled in to find an empty hook.

Dad wasn't much of a fisherman. But I suspect he knew just what he was doing that summer morning—and it wasn't simply teaching me to fish. Oh, I was hooked all right—that bobber's first dance step ignited in me a passion for fishing that persists undampened to this day and has drawn me to some of the world's most exotic waters from Alaska to the Caribbean and Hawaii. But I think Dad's goal that day was more ambitious and vital—he wanted me to begin to see my own spirituality, to understand what faith is, to sense the unfathomable meaning of God. Pretty heady stuff for a six-year-old!

I think—therefore I am. I eat—therefore I grow. We're always involved with the mental and physical aspects of our humanity. But we are spiritual beings as well, and that aspect is often the neglected stepchild of our nature, not well developed or nurtured. I am somewhat biased, of course, but I've come to believe that fisherpersons are blessed with special opportunities to sense the spiritual, to believe in worlds they can't see, to "catch" God—and vice versa.

Since you've stayed with me this far, I invite you to come along on a different kind of angling odyssey. We probably won't get into a whale's belly, a la Jonah, but we might visit the Sea of Galilee and a trout stream or two, cast a fly and a plug and maybe some bread on the waters, meet some fishermen named Peter and James and Homer and Cotton, and eat a very special meal or two. I'll tell you up front that we'll be following the lead of a carpenter, not a fisherman (although, hang in with me a bit longer and you may be convinced otherwise), because this is my story and I believe in a Christian God, the Father of us all. But there are many avenues and ideas that lead to God. Hitch up your chest waders, line up your own perceptions of the Almighty, and let's head out.

Chapter 1

WHERE TO GO

M ost of us afflicted with the piscatorial urge have two or three species that we favor, and they largely determine the kinds of waters we fish. I am drawn to trout and smallmouth bass, partly because of their elegant good looks and fighting ability, but mostly because of the places they live. Not long after this is written, I will hike into the mountains of Virginia's Shenandoah National Park to one of the laughing little headwaters streams that tumble in white froth from pool to pool, their jade waters reflecting the lush hardwood forests that hem them in and love to snag a fisherman's fly. If my casts are true, each pool will yield at least one native brook trout with white-edged fins and jewellike markings on its dark back. Far too beautiful to kill, each will be freed from the barbless hook and released gently back into the clean, air-clear waters from which it came.

A mid-April morning in this place—with the sun's slanting rays illuminating the light green leaves of reborn forest, the brilliant white blooms of dogwoods, and the achingly beautiful redbud trees—is far more than a fishing trip. It's a resurrection, a lifting free of oneself and all the trappings and travail of day-to-day humanity. In their place is an incredible quieting, a chance for the mind to purge and the soul to listen for the still, small voice of God.

If you are just getting started in fishing and trying to decide where to go, conjure up the kinds of natural settings that make you feel good. Maybe it's standing in the booming surf as the sun boils up over the horizon or plummets into a blood-red sea, gulls screaming and wheeling all around. Or riding a bouncing drift boat down a brawling western river. Or sitting on the shore of a big southern impoundment, a canepole propped up in a forked stick. You might catch something or you might not. But you'll find peace, and where there is peace, there is God.

The following few offerings may give you a taste of what's in store for those who fish in places ranging from Virginia and Florida to Hawaii.

Though not a native Virginian, I've lived here for almost four decades, and I am enamored of the James and New rivers. Not only do they drain much of the land mass of this state, but both nurture rich populations of sky-busting smallmouth bass that draw fishermen from all over the mid-Atlantic region. Their differences are striking: Float the New and you can almost sense that something is different here. This ancient river system in southwest Virginia is geologically the third oldest in the world, and the only nontidal river in the East that flows northward and crosses the Appalachian Mountains. Throughout its journey the New River meanders through spectacular mountain scenery complete with craggy cliffs and magnificent gorges. Several major Class II and III rapids keep rafters and canoeists paying attention. The James is not so feisty, but it is one very long and lush blue line, flowing 348 miles from the confluence of the Cowpasture and Jackson rivers in central Virginia all the way to Chesapeake Bay.

Rick casts from an island campsite.

Riverdreams

Two left feet push in unison against the foot of the boat ramp; there's a brief squealing protest of aluminum against concrete, and then we are no longer tethered to the land. The river gathers us in, and we more than willingly surrender to her pull.

After thirty-five years of deadlines and directives, giving up control does not come easily to either the captain or the first mate of our eighteen-foot canoe. But we've been here before, and we know that over the next three days Virginia's James River will minister kindly to us—unless we do something stupid. She is a fecund and dignified river, usually well-behaved in spring and summer, but she does not suffer fools well. She will not look kindly, for example, on a visitor who holds a spinning rod sideways in his teeth while paddling furiously upstream against the current to free a bottom-snagged lure.

Fishing is the main reason Rick and I come here each year—usually in May, though the James is user-friendly from April to October. If conditions are right, it's no trick to catch 100 fish a day per angler. The major quarries are smallmouth bass, one of the strongest of all freshwater fighters, and hand-size-plus long-ear sunfish. Taken on ultralight spinning tackle or fly rods, they are delightful adversaries.

But their greatest attraction comes at day's end, when they sizzle in butter in a long-handled frypan, bought at a yardsale for a dollar. My partner, a master at campfire cooking, outdoes himself this year, and we eat until we can eat no more.

Sated and sipping a Corona with lime wedge, we sit on a weathered old flood-debris tree that our hostess the river seems to have placed here in this idyllic place for our personal edification. A half-nickel moon lays a path of molten silver across the whispering river to our island campsite.

Staring into the always changing campfire, we talk about important things like family, and the future, and fears, and God. And we revel in the plu-perfect pleasure of simply being here. We shake our heads at the fact that in the seventeen miles of river we will float by tomorrow noon, we will have seen only two other boats— four other people—this on one of the East's major rivers that drains almost the entire state of Virginia, an hour from Roanoke, two from Richmond, three from Washington, DC.

Flat-out gone are worries, stresses, problems. In their place are such river delights as the female wood duck fluttering across the surface in the broken-wing ploy while her downy newborn offspring splatter off in the opposite direction . . . staggering out of our little tent at four a.m. to see a sky ablaze with stars, including the Gemini Twins, Castor and Pollux (we dub them Castor and Oil) . . . the sight of a buster smallmouth soaring two feet above the surface, his tail a butterfly blur in the bright sunlight as he disdainfully throws a lure back at me.

Our three-day odyssey ends too soon, but it leaves with both of us a subliminal record of river dreams to be called to mind whenever the gargoyles of modern living start catching up to us.

Angler on a Roll: Part 1

No, this article will not describe how to prepare your favorite fisherman so that he or she looks good cooked up hamburger-style and served on a dinner plate. It will, rather, detail one of the best weeks of fishing in my entire misbegotten life, and wind up with a quick and easy way to grill a whole fish so that it's juicy, smoky, and luscious.

Over Memorial Day weekend, older son Kevin and grandboys Grayson (then ten) and Devin (seven) and I camped out with another family on a grassy section of bank flanking the New River not far from Blacksburg, Virginia. The weather was outstanding, and we were looking forward to the maiden voyage of a canoe Kevin and I had just bought.

The New is among Virginia's top rivers for smallmouth bass and we had brought our tackle, but I wasn't expecting much—the river is nearly a quarter-mile wide there and generally pretty shallow, and lots of other outdoor-minded people were camped in the area.

After dinner Sunday evening, the crew of the Rooneytania set sail, Kev and I paddling in stern and bow, two young gentlemen sharing the center seat, and fishing rods bristling upward. Dusk was building, and I could see we would have no more than an hour to fish.

Most of us were casting something called a Crickhopper, a two-inch floating/diving lure that's about the best overall attractor I've ever used for smallmouths in this area. We hadn't been at it more than ten minutes when something with shoulders grabbed the tightly wiggling lure and began taking out line. My little ultralight spinning rod was truly straining its onions when a fine bass tore through the surface and shook its tail at us before crashing back in. The lure's small hooks held, and a few minutes later the three-pounder was on a stringer attached to the canoe's center thwart.

Between casts, the boys couldn't keep their eyes off that lively bass swimming on the stringer a foot below the surface. We named him Fred (after my best fishing buddy, whom you will meet later in this book).

Fast-forward an hour or so. Now it's close to full dark and we're only about a hundred feet offshore and heading for the campsite. We'd caught a few other, small fish, but now we were all ready to collapse around the campfire.

Wally's in the boat!

Last cast, I said to myself as I flipped the Crickhopper toward shore. Well, I must have hit that unseen leviathan right about on the head, because as soon as that bit of plastic splashed down, it disappeared in a whirlpool the size of your biggest frypan. In water that couldn't have been any deeper than a foot and a half, something hulking pushed a bow wave as it headed for more substantial depths.

"What in the world is this?" I said aloud (or words to that effect). The boys were shouting, the reel was screaming, and I was just holding on for dear life as that creature wallowed around somewhere out there in the near-dark.

I could go on and on (and have, many times, since then), but thankfully I wrestled that fish to the boat, lifted it aboard by the lower lip, and held it up for the world to see—all five pounds of it. It was close to the biggest smallmouth bass I've ever taken.

This one, given the name Wally, went on the stringer next to Fred, dwarfing him and making him sulk. The kids loved it. Wally and Fred thereby joined the short list of priceless piscatorial portraits that prowl the backroads of what's left of my mind.

The next morning, still feisty and flopping on their stringer, they were dispatched, iced down, and brought to my home port of Buena

Vista. The accompanying sidebar highlights the final act in this little drama.

But I ain't done yet! See the article below the sidebar.

Best Way To Grill a Whole Fish

If you can't bring yourself to reduce your catch to fillets, here's a surefire way to grill an entire fish (or two or three) intact—with the innards removed, of course—and ensure that its skin will be crisp and its flesh moist.

- In each side, make three deep cuts paralleling the rib bones. Rub both sides with oil (vegetable, not olive, oil), then salt and pepper to taste.
- Clean your grill well, preheat it on hot, then turn it down to medium.
- Place the fish on one side, uncovered. Wait five minutes, then use tongs to pry it gently from the grill, taking care to free the flesh wherever it may stick to the hot metal. Put it down on the other side and cook for two to three minutes longer.
- Gently roll the critter over, using a metal spatula. Cook for up to ten minutes longer, depending on how big the fish is. Check for doneness by probing the three deep cuts you made with a knife. The flesh should appear opaque.
- When it's done, sprinkle on some chipotle powder—naw, just kidding, lemon juice will do—and serve.

Angler on a Roll: Part 2

It is now just four days after the saga of our family's encounter with Wally and Fred. Thanks to a couple of young'uns who were eyeball witnesses, that story is likely still circulating—around Blacksburg anyway.

In late May and early June, the fancy and fantasies of most freshwater fishermen are focused on either bass or trout. Having pushed my luck with the smallmouths, I decided to head for a different kind of honey hole not far from home, this one offering one of the aristocrats of gamefish, the photogenic rainbow trout. I've always been partial to these handsome, hard-fighting fish—largely because they mostly live in hilly to mountainous areas that we humans haven't yet beaten into submission.

When Rita (AKA Dear Spouse) and I moved to the hills of central Virginia a half dozen years earlier (2006), John Roberts, a local trout chaser of the first order, generously briefed me on this area's best bets for rainbow, brook, and brown trout. One of them was a place called Hidden Valley, about an hour's drive to the west. Through it runs the Jackson River, certainly one of the mid-Atlantic's most attractive streams.

I had first visited the Jackson the previous spring, mostly to check it out, though I did take a few average-size trout on flies. But I learned something that day: Many miles of the river, winding along the foot of a series of mountains in the Washington-Jefferson National Forest, are stocked with fish by the state. It's a long way between access points, which means you have to be willing to hump for miles along an old rutted lane to get to the best fishing.

Or you can use a bicycle. The lane is inaccessible to motorized vehicles, but on that initial visit I saw a few guys peddling along, and found their bikes leaning against trees as I fished my way upstream.

My folks didn't raise any dumb kids—at least that's what my five sisters and I keep telling each other—so early on a superb May morning I jammed my old bike into the Cherokee along with fly-fishing gear and lunch and headed for the hills. The Hidden Valley parking area had a few cars, but I was confident as I donned my fishing vest and a backpack, mounted up on the two-wheeler, and bumped up the lane into the forest, my creaky old near-septuagenarian carcass complaining most of the way.

It was a warm day at home, but up there in the shade it was comfortable. When I reached an attractive stretch of deep, riffly water that I judged was upstream of most of the other fishermen, I parked the bike, switched the sneakers for a pair of metal-cleated wading shoes, tied on a No. 14 green nymph, and waded out in the cool, clear water.

Just being in this delightful wild place was pure pleasure, but it would soon get better. Working a weighted nymph on a light tapered leader involves drifting the fly close to the bottom and making it look as natural as possible, without "drag" caused by the current.

The biggest challenge, though, is detecting strikes, which are usually as subtle as a minuscule twitch of the line where it enters the water.

A fine rainbow from the Jackson River.

On my third cast, as the fly swung around downstream at the end of the drift, something yanked on the line as if trying to win a tug of war. So much for subtle. I didn't have to strike back—he'd hooked himself. Almost immediately he soared up into the sunlight, flinging water and reflecting diamonds, before crashing back in to slug it out with me.

The nine-foot graphite rod soon sapped the strength of the surging trout, and I brought him to hand—fourteen and a half inches, a keeper for sure. I waded to shore, killed him quickly, gutted him, and put him into a bag lined with moist green leaves from the shoreside vegetation to keep him as cool as possible.

Other, more modest rainbows and one little brook trout came to hand that morning and were released before I parked my old carc on a streamside boulder to relax and eat lunch. A gentle breeze made the leaves whisper conspiratorially, a vortex of yellow butterflies congregated in a little patch of sunlight, a snake ruddered slowly downstream. Dunno what I did to deserve this day and this place, but I thanked the Big Guy for all of it.

Farther up along the river is a multi-mile stretch governed by special fishing regulations: artificial lures only (no bait) and a catch limit of two fish sixteen inches or longer. I'd never gone up there, but I couldn't resist.

Leaving the bike hidden in some weeds, I started plodding upstream. After about twenty minutes I found a place that fairly shouted TROUT. The stream narrowed, forcing the water through a noisy chute and then into a deep run up against a sheer rock wall on the far side. The sun was casting long shadows already, and I decided this would be my last stop.

Where the chute ended and the water deepened and widened, I added a small split-shot to get the fly down and then made a cast. I *knew* it was going to happen: The fly stopped as if snagged on a deep rock. But then the pounding began as the fish, obviously heavy and swimming powerfully and ponderously, rumbled out into the fast water. Unseen and unstoppable, he headed downstream, taking all the slack line I was holding in my left hand and making the reel buzz as more line peeled off.

Praying the little hook would hold, I just held on and hoped he would tire sometime in my lifetime. The rod bent double as the piscatorial equivalent of an NFL linebacker, finally visible, made a last-ditch dash for an underwater branch. He fell just short, and soon was in the shallows at my feet. At sixteen and a half inches, he just made the cut, and joined his near-twin in my backpack.

My memorable week of great sport ended that evening, when Rita and I dined on grilled rainbow stuffed with artichokes. Life is good.

Hill-Country Bronzebacks

Some call it simply Southwest. Bass fishermen call it simply heaven. It's that triangular area of far western Virginia roughly enclosed between Cumberland Gap on the west and the New River on the east, and bordering on Kentucky, Tennessee, and North Carolina. If life is ever kind enough, I'll spend an entire springtime touching down like a dancing Mayfly on the best of the bass-rich waters in this rolling, rural "golden triangle."

The smallmouth—affectionately known as the bronzeback—is the king of gamefish here, and he wears his crown most regally not in lakes but in the rivers that separate and define the mountains that dominate this country. Most of those rivers flow from northeast to southwest. The one exception is the misnamed New, oldest river in the entire East and the only one in the region that runs north, cutting through the mountain ranges.

The New works its way out of North Carolina headwaters and is a broad-shouldered hulk of a river throughout most of its Virginia section, slowing only to accommodate sprawling Claytor Lake. The New supports heavy populations of bronzebacks both above and below the lake, but according to Richard Graham of Blacksburg, it is fished a bit harder between the lake and the West Virginia border. He recommends the twenty-mile stretch upstream of the town of Galax. The river is smaller here and fairly shallow, but in May and early June—which Graham says is prime time for the New—the top-water sport is superb.

The river is deeper between Galax and Claytor Lake, and some of the best fishing in its entire flow is in the fifteen miles above the big lake. The problem here is access. It's all private property, and there are few roads. One solution could be to put a johnboat or canoe in at the Shot Tower, a landmark along Rt. 52, and floatfish your way down to Rt. 100 or the lake itself.

That brings up a point to remember about all the rivers in Southwest: you can wade-fish in some places, but generally the best way to reach the lightest-fished areas is to float them in a small boat. Virginia's Department of Game and Inland Fisheries (DGIF) has a wealth of detailed information about access points and launch places, especially for sizable rivers like the New and James.

Here's a "thumbsucker": If largemouth bass are your pleasure, try the three or four miles of the New around the White Thorn boat landing. For some reason, the bigmouths almost outnumber the smallies here.

To the west of the New are the three forks of the Holston River, and the best of them is the North Fork. Be forewarned that the state has in the past warned anglers not to eat fish from this stretch because of mercury leaching into the water from a mine nearby. But small-mouths are there in substantial numbers.

Paralleling the North Fork about twenty miles farther west is the Clinch River. In the upper half of Virginia's ninety-five-mile stretch above St. Paul this river reels like a drunken sailor, and its twistings create holes and runs and ledges and bouldered white water that make a bronzeback angler salivate. The Clinch is a floatfisherman's dream, and not a single dam interrupts its flow. A "slot" limit is in effect on the Clinch—you can't keep any bass between eleven and fourteen inches long.

Jump-off Places

Here are a couple of excellent choices in places to headquarter while you check out the fishing in Southwest.

The family will love you if you take them to Mountain Lake, a 2,600-acre mountaintop resort near Blacksburg. Open from early spring to late November, the resort features fine dining and superb scenery and hiking. Drought and other causes have severely shrunk the twenty-seven-acre lake there, but it is undergoing restoration.

Farther west, the little city of Wytheville is centrally located for fishing both the upstream stretches of the New River as well as the Holston, Clinch, and other rivers of Southwest. It has a Holiday Inn and many other reasonably priced hotels, and many local attractions are nearby.

How do you catch the bronzebacks in the rivers of this rumpled land? It really isn't very difficult—unless the water is high and relatively cold, which it can be in early and mid May. If those conditions prevail, the very best tactic is to work big natural baits—madtoms, crawfish, hellgrammites, and big shiners—very slowly along the bottom in the deepest holes. Some buster smallmouths are taken this way. Flyfishermen should work big streamers down low on high-density sinking lines. In lures, choose marabou jigs and quarter-ounce or larger crankbaits.

As the water warms, the fishing gets more genteel—and productive. The bass—perhaps wanting a closer look at the lush-blooming dogwoods and mountain laurel and wild azalea—begin feeding ever shallower. To my mind, nothing beats the visual thrill of a smallmouth bass busting a surface lure, and a day's float on one of these rivers can dish up a hundred such strikes.

A Can't-Miss Lure

When the weather warms enough for terrestrial critters to begin lurking in the eddies, the bass in these Virginia rivers will all but turn themselves inside out for a small lure dubbed the Crickhopper. Just a couple of inches long (a larger version is also available) and weighing a tenth of an ounce, the grasshopper/cricket combination gives the user lots of options: It can be manipulated on the surface to act like the real thing. If that doesn't draw a strike, the lure has a lip that allows an enticing, tight-wiggle underwater retrieve.

On the New and other rivers, I've had bass, bull bluegills, and even a walleye charge this insistent little creation and either hook themselves or knock the thing into the air in their enthusiasm. The lure is available is yellow grasshopper (my favorite), green grasshopper, black cricket, brown cricket, and other finishes.

Use smallish surface lures including the Crickhopper, Rebels and Rapalas, or go sub-surface with curlytail jigs, shallow-running crankbaits, and buzzbaits, especially versions with clear blades. Flyfishermen should work small poppers and deerhair bugs. Richard Graham recommends the Sneaky Pete, a bullet-shaped cork bug with rubber legs, fished almost without any motion besides the current's.

Another thumbsucker: Toss out a bass lure in the New or Clinch rivers, and it may come back clenched in the toothy jaws of a muskellunge. Hang one of these prodigious predators, and he will definitely make your day! A map is available that pinpoints the Clinch's best muskie stretches and also shows all the boat-launching spots along the river. Go for it!

However you fish these delightful rivers, they will make you feel like a king—with a crown made of bronze.

Hawaiifish!

**This remote, romantic, graceful group of
islands is the stuff of movie legends,
but it can also conjure up lots of fishing fantasies.**

I didn't go to Hawaii for the fishing. I went to experience the
drive-in volcanoes, the thousand-foot waterfalls of Kauai's Na
Pali Coast, the Seven Pools of Kipahulu on the island of Maui.
But in this land of exotic superlatives, the sea and its abundant life
always beckon, and my wife Rita and I were blessed to be able to
answer the call.

Aboard our sleek fishing craft, trolling slowly along the Kohala
Coast off the Big Island of Hawaii, I looked beyond the white wake
gleaming astern to the point where 13,800-foot Mauna Kea shoul-
dered up into and above a cloud bank. Beyond the bow and clearly
visible, despite its thirty-mile distance, was 10,000-foot Mount
Haleakala, across the strait on the island of Maui. I rose from my
comfortable seat and peered down into the incredibly blue water, of
a clarity I've never seen in continental North America. And I marveled that life can be this graceful.

Such is the essence of fishing in Hawaii, geographically one of
the world's most isolated island chains. That isolation is both a prime
attraction for visitors and a reason for the diversity of Hawaii's underwater life.

You can sail aboard a blue-water cruiser and within minutes be
struggling with a blue marlin weighing several hundred pounds. That
same afternoon you can drop a bait down to the bottom on light line
and a whippy rod and catch reef species in a riot of colors that would
make a snorkeler proud.

Hawaii's most dramatic and challenging fishing is done aboard
the Hatteras-style and other charter boats that sail out of Kailua-
Kona on the Big Island of Hawaii, which with some justification calls
itself the marlin capital of the world. When Rita and I were there in
mid-May, more than 850 marlin—most of them blues—already had
been boated since the first of the year by charters out of Kona alone.

One of Hawaii's oddball offerings.

Imagine it's your turn in the fighting chair, and the skipper up on the flying bridge above you yells, "Fin off port rigger!" Translated from the original anglerese, that means a marlin has come up behind the bait or lure being trolled from the rod whose line is held off to the left side of the boat by an outrigger, or long fiberglass pole. This husky ocean-roaming gamefish will try to stun a bait by slapping it with a sideways thrust of its long bill. It may grab the bait then, but often it turns away maddeningly and may or may not make another pass to claim the prize.

You are strapped into the fighting chair, and the rod butt is positioned in a swiveling mount between your legs. You are very much aware that in the next few seconds you may be directly attached via a wispy-looking line to a rampaging hulk that's likely to weigh more than you and your best friend put together. (The largest blue marlin taken in Hawaiian waters weighed 1,805 pounds, and they normally weigh 300 to 400 pounds.)

That knowledge arouses mixed emotions—you're not sure you really want the fish to strike. But it takes the bait solidly, and you rear back on the rod two, three, four times—as hard as you can— to set the hook. The next few minutes are a blur as the streamlined gamester races across the surface in a series of leaps that leave you bug-eyed and gasping.

Then the "reel" work begins—pumping and reeling, pumping and reeling, only to lose all or most of the line you gained when the fish goes off on another tear. If you persevere and bring it to boat-side, your back and arms will hurt—guaranteed. But you will feel euphoric too. You'll have taken on the king of the billfish and bested it on sporting tackle.

And now it's decision time. If you have the soul of a conservationist, you'll instruct the mate to release the fish—perhaps with a tag attached to it for study. If you have a specific use for the fish—mounting, selling, or filling your freezer—it will be brought aboard or towed to the dock for show and tell.

It's a good idea to discuss this with your captain before you leave the dock. A charter boatman's best advertising is the catch hung up at the dock for pictures. Big billfish always draw a crowd and can generate business. So some captains don't take kindly to the catch-and-release concept. The fish themselves, however, are reported to be crazy about it.

After you've tangled with a marlin, Hawaii's lesser gamefish may seem, well, lesser. But there's nothing second-rate about wahoo (known locally as *ono*), bar-marked torpedoes weighing up to forty pounds that roam over deep-sea ledges where the bottom drops off sharply. Or yellowfin tuna (called *ahi*), hard fighters that may top 300 pounds. Or dolphin (*mahi-mahi*)—no, not Flipper but the fish with the blunt head and iridescent green-and-yellow markings, one of the most striking denizens of any ocean anywhere.

All of those are usually caught by the trolling technique from blue-water charter boats, which can be pricey. But excellent and less expensive fishing trips are found on the island of Maui, just a commuter hop from the Big Island. For a fraction of the charterboat fee I reserved a spot on the comfortable Excel, a forty-three-foot Delta that docks in the village of Maalaea at the "waist" of this voluptuous island. As you sail seaward for six hours of fishing, the gods of 10,000-foot Mount Haleakala are said to shepherd you. You won't get your money back if you don't catch fish—but you'll catch fish. The boat offers a combination of trolling for the large open-water species and bottom-fishing for the myriad species that live on the reefs.

My day aboard the Excel started when I dropped a sandwich overboard trying to clamber toward the fighting chair as something grabbed a trolled lure and set the reel screaming. I needn't have hurried—it wasn't my turn. (In trolling for the large species, only one customer at a time fights a fish.) But all hands were pulling for the fisherman, who got the thrill of his twelve years as he worked a thirty-pound wahoo to boatside.

In early afternoon the captain stopped the boat over a deep reef and passed out the lighter fishing outfits. The guarantee was fulfilled in the next hour as all eight of us scored repeatedly.

Crevalle Creativity

The same light tackle used for bottomfishing has another application that a few Hawaiian skippers know about. "Whipping" is essentially a system of working surface lures—and sometimes spoons and jigs—over shallow reefs for jack crevalle (called *papio*), blue crevalle (*omilu*), and giant trevally (*ulua*).

When I was there, veteran charter-boat skipper Ken Takashima took his whipping clients across the strait to the "pineapple island" of Lanai, where coral reefs and crumbling cliff areas provide lots of fish-holding bottom rubble. He used felt-tip marking crayons to paint his surface lures black, which he says is by far the most productive color most of the time. You toss a lure up into the white water crashing on shore or over a visible reef and retrieve it with a noisy, churning retrieve. Watching these husky fish blast the lure on top is a real charge.

The best months for whipping are June through August, but the fish can be caught year-round.

The best part was not knowing what might materialize as we winched our adversaries up through 120 feet of shimmering water. Sometimes it was a serving-platter-sized *palani* (surgeonfish), blue and yellow and buck-toothed. Or a blue-stripe snapper. Or a pure-gold, foot-long creature whose name I never did discover, so awed was I by its coloration.

Or a spiny pufferfish, much like what East Coast U.S. fishermen call a blowfish. Tickle its belly and it inflates grotesquely into a shape a quarterback could throw sixty yards. In markets here it is sometimes called sea squab. The Japanese pay $50 for a meal of the Pacific version, which they call *fuku* (and which must be cleaned and cooked just so, or it can poison the gourmet).

You don't even need a boat to enjoy some of Hawaii's fishing. If you borrow, beg, or bring along a sturdy casting outfit (a surf rod and reel are ideal), you can catch a variety of species right from the shore. Local store owners and hotel employees on all the islands can point you to the right places.

Such as the flower-bedecked island of Kauai, where fishermen toss baits seaward within the spray reach of Spouting Horn, a geyser that bursts out of an ancient lava tube to the rhythm of the pulsing sea. You'll find the spot at the end of the Lawai Road near the town of Poipu.

And on Maui there's Waianapanapa State Park on the superb Road to Hana. Here the surging sea has sculpted the toe of an old lava flow into fluted black columns, jagged cliffs, and craggy caves through which the swells crash.

I didn't catch anything there. Maybe that's because it was hard to concentrate on fishing in that captivating place of white water blasting against black lava, bikinis on a black-sand beach, and lush rainforest vegetation in a variety of greens enriched by the low sun and clean air.

Disneyfish!

**The attractions of this world-famous
resort will fire up Mom, the kids, and anybody
who loves lunker largemouths.**

It's mid-February. The snow and ice that entomb the world outside the den window seem also to have a grip on your psyche—
we outdoor types suffer a special form of cabin fever—and your
mind is conjuring images of misty, warm sunrises, drifting boats,
and leaping fish.

In the kitchen, your wife is preparing dinner and conjuring up her
own brand of leisure-time dreams—flying off to a villa somewhere
to the south, shopping in exotic stores, sightseeing, gallery-hopping.
The kids are parked in front of the TV, which keeps reminding them
that they can fly south for about the price of a good snow shovel, and
what they want is junk food and an amusement park.

How in the world, you wonder, does a fisherman/husband/father
plan a vacation that will fulfill everyone's wish list? Is it worth trying
to pull off, or will such a trip end up with none of the family members really satisfied?

I'll admit that I had my doubts. But I'm here to state that it can
indeed be done—and without breaking the family bank account. And
the rewards of exposing youngsters to the sport of fishing and the
natural world around them can make your trip a whole lot more than
just a vacation.

It was mid-June when the Rooney clan—my wife Rita; Brian,
nine; Kristin, seven; and I—took advantage of bargain summer air-
fares and flew to Miami, where we rented a compact car and drove
to the central Keys for a three-day stay at a wonderful resort called
Hawk's Cay near the fishing village of Marathon. There we lazed
around in tropical splendor—part of which included a complimentary
breakfast buffet that included everything from corn flakes to lamb
chops. Brian and I got into a training pen with six dolphins, which
allowed us to take hold of their dorsal fins and get a ride neither of
us will forget.

And of course Dad managed to line up two fishing trips out of the resort's eighty-five-slip marina—one for bonefish with a veteran guide and one for tarpon with that guide's son. Because of some rough weather, we didn't reduce the fish populations appreciably, but more good things were to come.

A leisurely six-hour run up the Florida Turnpike brought us to the Kissimmee-St. Cloud area, home of Disney World. The kids were bouncing off the walls with anticipation, and I'll admit I was fired up myself. Disney World is located amid some of the finest largemouth bass fishing in the entire U.S. Within a radius of forty miles are such "hawg"-holding waters as Lakes Tohopekaliga, Cypress, Hatchineha, and Kissimmee (the Kissimmee chain); the Harris chain north of Disney World; the Clermont chain to the west; the St. Johns River, and dozens of others. Not to mention the waters on Disney World property itself—about which more later.

Mom was pleased too when we walked into our "villa," a two-story, two-bedroom, fully equipped townhouse at Fantasy World Club Villas, just three miles from the entrance to the Magic Kingdom. Very well equipped, lanai on the back porch, daily maid service, "floating driving range," kids splash pools—this wasn't your typical strip-development motel or fishing-camp accommodations.

At 5:15 the next morning I met fishing guide John Lynn and we headed for sprawling Lake Tohopekaliga. Fifteen minutes later, we were pushing his bass boat off the trailer and into fog-enshrouded shallows. This big, affable fellow knows these shallow lakes like he knows his backyard. He picked Toho—as everybody calls it—because it was still in the throes of a drawdown and the fish were holding in the deeper areas and thus a bit easier to find.

We eased up to within casting range of a patch of mostly submerged treetops that seemed to float disembodied between water and mist, and began tossing white spinnerbaits. The structure, he told me, had been placed by the Florida Game and Fresh Water Fish Commission expressly to provide cover for gamefish, and I saw immediately that it was doing just that: bass were sucking and slurping and slashing at the surface as they chased baitfish. And some of those fish had shoulders on them. John hooked one that would not be horsed despite his husky rod and seventeen-pound-test line—it bulled back into the stickups, tangled the line, and broke off.

As the fog began to yield to the sun, which is fierce here in summer and puts the fish down and off their feed, the guide suggested we try one more spot before it got too hot to fish. His 125-horse outboard rumbled throatily as we meandered a few hundred yards to an expanse of water that looked exactly like all the rest of the surface that was beginning to become visible. He cut the motor over what they call a dropoff in Florida—a spot where the water deepens from two or three feet over a bar to "depths" of five or six.

"I've taken some real hawgs here," the guide said, using the ubiquitous term for lunker largemouths in the South. I thought we'd be rigging up with large shiners—that's the way many anglers here fish for big bass, I knew. But John handed me a Rattletrap lure, a crankbait with beads inside that vibrates and rattles on the retrieve. We'd need the extra attractor abilities because of the murky waters, he told me. He uses big live baits in the winter, November through March, when the large bass hit better than they do in summer. He told me his clients take a largemouth of ten pounds or better on the average of every five days during that period. I've been fishing since age six and had never caught a bass half that size.

After tossing the Rattletrap for about fifteen minutes, I was wool-gathering a bit when something climbed all over that lure. I struck hard and hooked it, but it didn't seem like much of a fish; it came meekly toward the boat and, rather than darting and diving like a typical bass, moved slowly and rather ponderously. When it got close, I snubbed it up, figuring to get a quick lip hold and let it go. But it wouldn't snub! It made a half-left and just kept swimming as the drag on my reel squealed. About thirty feet out, it wallowed on top and managed to launch about three-quarters of its bulk out of the water—no mean feat in that summer-hot liquid—and I could only gape at its size and say a small prayer of thanks that John had insisted I put away my eight-pound-test rig that I'd brought from home and use his heavier outfit.

First fish I ever kissed. She deserved it.

That pot-bellied old female largemouth weighed nine pounds two ounces and was twenty-six and a quarter inches long, by far the largest I have ever caught. I couldn't resist giving her a smootch right on the lips as I released her to thrill some other angler.

Rather than boil our brains through the middle of the day, we both went home and relaxed, meeting again at 4 p.m. for a crack at another of John's "dropoffs." This time my son Brian joined us, as did John's brother Ross. We roared a couple of miles downlake, then eased overboard to wade and cast to fish that, John said, moved up on the bar to feed in late afternoon.

We hooked a few fish, but for me the highlight was watching Brian, who stayed aboard as Ross waded and pulled the boat slowly along the bar via a rope tied to his waist. Brian isn't as crazy about fishing as his old man is, and I was hoping our experiences in Florida would help to "sink the hook home." I watched as he cast from the bow and took in the natural panorama around him—a crane winging overhead, seeming to be all neck and legs; the lake's calm surface mirroring the kaleidoscopic cloud patterns in the sky; the half-wild cattle roaming freely on the distant shore. And the final mind-picture: a bald eagle wheeling gracefully against a blackening sky striped by a double rainbow. Shortly thereafter, the wind changed and the storm took after us and we were forced to scoot back to the landing.

I don't know whether Brian will remember that afternoon as vividly as the attractions we visited over the next few days, including the Magic Kingdom, Epcot Center, and Sea World, all within a twenty-minute drive of the Fantasy World Villas. But I know Rita and I will long remember the perspectives we got the morning we boarded a comfortable, canopied pontoon boat for a crack at the abundant bass in Bay Lake and the Seven Seas Lagoon on Disney World itself.

These guided trips are popular with vacationers like the Rooney clan who want to mix some fishing with their Disney visit. For a very reasonable fee, a group of up to five fisherpersons can board a roomy boat at the Fort Wilderness Campground and be squired to the best bass spots on the Disney lakes. The cost includes the services of a guide, tackle, lures, and coffee and soft drinks. The length of a trip is two to three hours.

We were lucky to be in the capable hands of a retiree who obviously loves this part-time work. He rigged up light outfits for Brian and Kris while Rita and I used tackle that I had brought along. My earlier guide, John, would have been horrified by my ultralight rig and six-pound-test line, but it was ideal for the "eating-size" largemouths we took that morning.

There was one exception: As we worked a weedy point hard against the ferryboat dock where millions of visitors first step onto the Magic Kingdom, something grabbed my black plastic worm and steamed away so powerfully that it broke the line almost before I had time to react.

Not that these lakes don't hold some real buster bass—bigmouths of up to fourteen pounds have been taken here. But this was summer, not the best time of year for fishing, and the larger bass tend to be lethargic and feed little once the sun gets up. The best fishing is from November through spring, and late March through May is the least-crowded time to visit the theme park. But it's also the time when the guided fishing trips book up weeks in advance. It's a good idea to make a reservation in advance of your trip.

Kris with her first Disneyfish. Mom and Brian approve.

I mentioned perspectives a bit earlier. One of them was watching six-year-old Krissie trying her darnedest to master the complexities of a spincast outfit, and then beaming as she reeled in a pan-size bass that leaped and cavorted on the surface. Another was Brian in his multicolored shorts (even at age nine, he likes to make a statement with his clothes!) holding a throbbing rod bent in an arc that seemed to frame Space Mountain in the background.

Yes, we had a great time in Florida, each of us in his or her own way. And there were some lessons learned too. As we released each fish we caught, as we boiled in the blazing sun and sped dockward ahead of a mean-looking storm, as we moved across the clean, clear, bass-rich lakes almost in the shadow of Cinderella's Castle and the throngs of people who wander there each year, each of us came to see a bit more clearly the single most important lesson offered by the natural world—that the freedom to take from that world brings with it the responsibility to conserve wisely its gifts of woods and water and wildlife.

Little Pleasures

The Maury, our "home" river, was muddy enough to plow, as they say around here, when I plodded along her banks on this summer morning. The thunderboomers and gullywashers we'd been having almost daily had done their damage. But it's a real chore to catch smallmouth bass in the confines of my home office, and I've long agreed with the old saw that a bad day fishing beats the pants off a good day working.

So I maneuvered out on a riverside boulder and began tossing a white curlytail jig. I couldn't see the lure until I'd reeled it back within four or five inches of the surface, which of course meant that the fish couldn't see the thing either. When the lure snagged an underwater obstacle on my fourth cast and I had to break the line, another saying came unbidden into what's left of my mind: "A fisherman is a jerk at one end of the line waiting for a jerk at the other." Dear Spouse loves that one.

As I meandered back toward my old brown Cherokee, however, purple thistle flowers, the sun bouncing diamonds off the still-wet foliage, and the water rolling brown at the base of a vertical gray cliff got me musing about the myriad little pleasures of living in Virginia's Rockbridge County and environs.

If you've lived here a while, maybe the sensory delights described below are old stuff. But spouse and I have only recently fled here from the warrens of northern Virginia and we are smitten by the likes of these local attractions:

**Yellow-flowered mullein,
without bluebird.**

Gotta make sure they're ripe.

**A hatchling song sparrow rides the
wind in a hanging flowerpot.**

- Did you know that dry pine cones make wonderful fire starters? You probably did, and so did we, but there's nothing like a summer campfire to help a person revert to us humans' earlier role as hunter/gatherers. And once the blaze is lit and casting its mesmerizing glow on the people gathered around, it draws us in and seems to envelop us with a sense of mystery and a looseness of tongue. Or maybe it's the beer.

- A walk with Sam, our yellow Lab and sidekick, regaled us with the sight of an eastern bluebird perched at the very top of a common mullein (*Verbascum thapsus*), a tall, stalky plant that most of us know as lamb's ear. The mullein is flaunting its yellow flowers now in fields and on roadsides seemingly everywhere, and the low early sun spotlighted the bird's blue against the plant's blooms. I had the little digital camera, but as I raised it to center the scene, of course, the bird took its leave.

- On the same walk, a whitetail deer browsing at the forest's edge caught a glimpse of Sam, which sent her hightailing across an open field. There are deer galore in this county, but I never tire of watching their graceful movements and marveling at their incredible alertness and their ability to live cheek by jowl with us humans, whose senses are wimpy and weak by comparison. And can you believe how *brown* these normally gray creatures become in summer? Seems to me to defy nature's concept of protective coloration.

- Just across the street from our home is a large patch of wild blackberries. In a week or three I will wander over there with a sizable pot and harvest and sample and sample and harvest. I will bleed profusely from the vicious, backward-curving thorns of the plants, but after all, the body needs to purge itself every once in a while. And the knobby little fruits will help to replenish my blood supply and supplement our diet with all sorts of beneficial nutrients. And they're free for the taking.

- Our front porch is graced by a battalion of hanging baskets overflowing with summer flowers. A couple of weeks ago I took them all down to give the blooms a good watering and in the process discovered in one a nest with four brownish, speckled, half-inch-long eggs. The parental units—a brace of song sparrows—don't seem to mind my occasional watering forays, and yesterday as I write this, the nest contained just three eggs plus a tiny glob of brownish fuzz with a head and two minuscule body extensions that we hope will soon allow the creature to soar where mere humans cannot follow. This one couldn't take off on me, so I immortalized it with my tiny camera before gently rehanging its swaying home. The adult sparrows will get used to the ladder I will place on the porch to record the rest of the brood's births.

After a few days the Maury was again fishable, and I sallied forth to seek some of the little pleasures that lurk unseen beneath its surface. Summer wade-fishing is a special pleasure because of its simplicity: You need no boat or fancy tackle. The cool water is a perfect antidote for the intense sun. You seldom see another soul. All you need are a lightweight spinning rod, a pocket-fitting box to carry lures, good wading shoes with metal cleats (plying the Maury is like walking on bowling balls), sunscreen, and sunglasses.

In three hours of tossing a white curlytail jig I hooked some sixty fish, most of them smallmouth bass six to eight inches long. All of those were released. Onto the little metal stringer carried in my other pocket went three larger bass, a couple of hand-size long-ear sunfish, and two fat rock bass.

Filleted, dipped in egg batter and Italian breadcrumbs, and fried fresh out of the river, those little pleasures were a superb gift from this rumpled, stream-crossed place in which we live.

Chapter 2

READING THE WATER

A ny angler worth his salt knows that before you start flailing away with lure or bait, you study the conditions to determine where the quarry is likely to be. A lake fisherman looks at the shoreline for signs of steep dropoffs, rocky points, and weedbeds that provide cover for bass or other gamefish. A stream angler studies the flow of currents and eddies to see how and where they'll deliver the natural creatures on which trout or salmon or bass or walleyes feed. Even Peter and James and John and the rest of the gang of gillnetters working the Sea of Galilee knew that their best chances were in the evening and at night, when small baitfish would come to the surface to feed, in turn attracting the bigger fish.

We're always looking for signs, we fisherfolk. Oh, in our technological brilliance we've created sonar-based fishfinders and other devices to reassure us that there really *is* something down there, and a fisherman astute at reading the natural indicators can get a pretty good handle on where the fish are holding. But it doesn't take a whole lot of fruitless casts to begin to doubt what all the gadgets and signs are saying.

Simon Peter, the "first fisherman" of the Sea of Galilee, must have felt downright skunked and frustrated the day Jesus walked up and asked him to put out into deep water and lower the nets for a catch. "We have worked hard all night and have not caught anything," Peter told his friend. "But because you say so, I will let down the nets." Surely Peter thought this was a hopeless exercise. But this man Christ had spent many nights in Peter's home, and Peter knew He was powerful and visionary. So he and his partners did as they were bid, and "They caught such a large number of fish that their nets began to break."

Talk about a blitz! Peter was so astonished that he fell to his knees and said, "Go away from me, Lord; I am a sinful man!"

Just *once,* I'd love to fill a boat to the point of sinking. Ain't gonna happen, probably, but that's okay. The vision of what's beneath the surface will keep me casting into that watery world I can't make out. And somehow, believing is enough. If it was good enough for Peter, it's good enough for me.

Seeing is believing, according to the old saw. The stories below in this chapter reflect some of the revelations, the discoveries that fisherpeople can experience and embrace as they pursue this special outdoor activity. As they mature in this activity—reading and understanding the signs, honing their decisions, increasing their enjoyment—they can come closer to believing in the source of their success.

Flee From the Wrath!

A trek to a remote lake recharges the personal batteries and reminds us of some basic truths about how we ought to consume the bounties of nature.

You won't read the lake's name here. Not that you'd recognize it. The lake is one of the least prepossessing of Ontario's quarter-million—a couple of miles long and a half mile wide, little more than a wide pause in the meandering flow of one of many rivers in the southern part of the province.

The fishing ranges from so-so to superb. The sudden appearance of northern pike, perhaps, or some other combination of factors has significantly reduced the populations of smallmouth bass, walleyes, and muskellunge since my first visit there some twenty-five years ago.

Fred and I hike the rutted trail from the woodcutter's home, where we had left our truck and piled our gear and food into an all-but-defunct two-wheel cart held together with baling wire and prayer. Behind us we can hear the growl of Carl's tractor as he hauls the cart along the old logging road. Crimson maples and sumac and golden hickories, highlighted here and there in the low afternoon sun, wave a greeting. And the peeling paper birches stand clean and white against the darker forest, sentinels marking the familiar way. These birches don't grow well in Virginia, where I live now, and I miss them.

**Vin, Fred, and Jack discuss world peace (or something)
at Ontario camp.**

We top the last knob at the end of the four-mile trek and through the trees glimpse sun glinting from wavelets, and the old sensations begin to drum inside as we hurry downhill to where the ancient boat is pulled up and tied on the lakeshore. The pressures of making a living and raising families have kept us away for four years, but everything is the same—the island with the cabin on it, the house-size rock where the two big smallmouths grabbed our frogs at almost the same moment and leaped in tandem, that place along the left shoreline where the unearthly sound of some animal screaming in the blackness of a starless night scared the bejaysus out of us....

The sights and smells and memories flooding back in are washing away the detritus of the "normal" world—the boss's words a couple of days earlier ("Can't give you much of a raise this year") ... the new car we need so badly ... the two college kids with the big tuition bills ... the small but persistent signs of the aging process.

**Fred displays a day's keepers, which
will soon be a small mountain of fillets.**

All such thoughts are flat-out gone. In their place is unabashed excitement—the anticipation of seeing some toothy creature knife up out of the lake's rocky depths to take a lure, its bronze flanks flashing in a breeze-brisk, sun-sparkling morning, each leap punctuated by shouts of unrestrained glee. It will happen tomorrow. I know it.

We load the old metal boat, crank up the little outboard, and push off into another world. This place is ours, in a way no material possession can be owned. We burble past Muskie Cove, where on another night Fred hooked a humongous fish that we saw only in silhouette as it leaped and threw the hook right at boatside.

Dusk is dimming a magenta sky as we reach the head of the lake and enter the feeder river for the mile-and-a-half run to the camp. My tastes run to mountains and white water, but this stretch of meandering stream, averaging no more than eighty feet across, stirs me. Fair numbers of fishermen and hunters and woodcutters come here, and hulking old logs on the bottom testify to the river's historic use as a timber highway.

A husky smallmouth on a perfect fall morning. Life is good.

So it's not *de facto* wilderness, certainly. But it's wild enough for me, and as we round a bend where the water deepens abruptly, I see the place where something (muskie? submarine?) grabbed my spinner and, with more power than anything I have ever hooked in fresh water, towed the boat slowly and steadily up and down that part of the river until the hasp on my snap swivel straightened out. I never saw that fish, but my imagination's picture of it is something I will carry with me into old age.

The V-wake of a swimming muskrat catches the last rays of daylight, pointing the way around the last bend to the camp. Four weather-bent, russet-colored structures with white trim—two cabins, a shed, and an ice house—cluster on a little forest-enveloped bench on the right bank, seeming as natural there as the creak of oarlocks.

But something's different—our hosts have made some changes in the past four years. A little dock makes it easier to unload the boat. And inside the main cabin we find propane lights and refrigerator. These improvements generate conflicting emotions: Voices from an age earlier than my own whisper of the wisdom of learning to do without modern conveniences like electricity—instead using fire for light and heat, Coleman stoves for cooking, and digging down through two feet of ice-house sawdust to reach hundred-pound blocks of ice cut out of the lake the previous winter.

Fred has no such hangups about accepting the new comforts of camp—he offers to cut some firewood in case I prefer to cook and sleep outside. I make a comment about the quality of his ancestry. Then I notice that some of the cabin windows have old sawblades nailed across them—protection against bears—and my worries about the intrusion of the modern world seem to subside.

Dinner that night is special: two thick steaks with all the trimmings and a bottle of wine. Fred does the honors. He and my other outdoor cronies won't let me near the cookstove, and for good reason—twenty miles from nowhere is not a good place to come down with ptomaine.

After dinner we raise beer cans in a toast to our hosts, two brothers from southern Ontario whom we had never met until recently. I knew their late uncle a generation ago, when I first came here, but since then our visits have been arranged by a phone call or two. They leave the key—and we leave the rent money—with Carl, the woodcutter. We're the only non-family members to use the camp, as far as I know. I remind myself never to violate that trust. It's a rare commodity these days.

In the glow of the propane lamp, I notice the sign, cut from some long-out-of-print poster and tacked to the rough walls of the cabin: "FLEE FROM THE WRATH!" I guess that's what we've done, Fred and I—escaped from the ratrace, the demands and pressures, the responsibilities. But I suspect that we are here not nearly so much to run away from something as because we are pulled toward something ...

Fred and I have been friends since high school. Our wives are the best of friends, and our kids like each other. A man is richly blessed who has one or two friends with whom he can be genuinely himself, with whom he can share both thoughts and feelings, a belly laugh, and maybe a tear or two.

And there is something about the outdoors in general and this place in particular that cements this special friendship. We two have come here to renew an old kinship with this place. The turns and widenings and wild things of this lake and river. The sunken logs that break shearpins and provide lairs for muskies and walleyes. The echoes of past trips that are all but audible as I gaze unseeing out the cabin window.

We are indeed drawn here. I feel that pull every time I look at the oil painting on my livingroom wall—an uncanny likeness of the view downriver from this cabin. Fred found the painting in a gallery somewhere and presented it to me one Christmas.

Something waits for us here. The next morning we go out to taste it, braced by birdsong and windsong in the bright woods. A two-mile hike along dim paths takes us to a pool on the river. Two waterfalls keep boats from reaching this place; we used to think that no one ever came here, but we've since found bootprints, and, once, a soda bottle.

No matter. The smallmouths are here by the hundreds. The first time we found this place, Fred and I stood on a lavalike rock outcropping, which points into the pool's depths like a finger saying "Fish here!" and caught a smallmouth bass on almost every cast for *four hours*.

The passage of four years hasn't changed anything—we stand on the rock ledge with light rods throbbing violently as twelve- to fifteen-inch smallies soar skyward, their tails a butterfly blur in the morning sun. How many situations have you encountered in which you can let your joy out in spontaneous whoops and grins and gestures, without feeling intimidated by the surroundings or people nearby?

When the action slows a little, I pull a camera from my backpack. In an effort to get the right composition for the shot—grinning angler, bent rod, white water feeding the pool—I back up so far that I nearly slip off the ledge and join the fish. My partner nearly does the same, but because of spasmodic laughter.

The photos we take are mostly for the benefit of family and friends. For Fred and me, the important details of this place are imprinted on the soul. They are there for instant replay, to be called up to sustain us whenever the alligators are gaining on us. This place is part of the fabric of who we are as men trying to stay sane and solvent in a shrink-wrapped society whose often mindless, grasping values are yammered at us incessantly by the TV and print media. It's an anchor, a lifeline to the *real* world.

In a couple of days we'll be heading back to what most people think is the real world. My wife will be glad to see me—and I her. She's the greatest gift the good Lord has ever given me, and there's nothing we can't talk about together. But she'll never really understand the part of me that needs this little chunk of wild country, why I need to return here every once in a while.

Fred understands. He and I will be back—next year, I hope. I'll return for all the reasons I've tried to tell about here. But it's more than that. I need to bring my sons here. The younger one, Brian, is thirteen, and growing up in an age that is losing contact with the natural world and its processes. More and more children in this nation are becoming insulated from that world; more and more of the next generation—the people who will be making the land-use decisions that will determine the fate of wild country like this place—are growing up believing that milk comes from a plastic jig, that eating wild animals is unthinkable, that getting dirt under the fingernails as you plant a tree or a garden is something people used to do a long time ago.

Kids learn by experience. Brian needs to know—before the "real" world gets its hooks too firmly into him—what it feels like to stand in the wilderness on an inky night and be unable to see *anything*. He has to experience the taste of walleyes taken fresh from the water he can see from the cabin as he eats, and understand that it is fare no restaurant in the world can duplicate. He needs to know first-hand that nature can be cruel and unforgiving one day, benign and giving the next. And he must understand that the freedom to take from the natural world brings with it the responsibility to conserve its gifts of woods and water and wildlife.

If he learns those lessons, surely he'll have a step on the world when he too must face its wrath.

What Happens at the Camp ...

The classic ending to the above adage is: "... stays at the camp." The rationale is sound: it prevents visits by the police or game wardens, wards off wifely diatribes, and allows the participants to maintain their dignity and upright posture, so to speak. These days, my fisherfriends and I are too long in the tooth to make much of a ruckus. But back in our heydays, some "untoward" events took place. I hope I don't violate the adage by telling these true tales:

At my age it's hard to remember what happened fifteen minutes ago, but I recall with great fondness my first trip to this lake and river system about two and a half hours north of the Thousand Islands customs station on the New York/Ontario border. It took place in 1962, and fanned into a flaming inferno my smoldering love of wild places and wild creatures.

Just a few years ago we were heading up there after a hiatus of four years, the longest dry spell in that entire span of time. This year we were only three in total: New Jerseyan Fred Bekiarian and I have been friends since high school; Jack Burke has been my bud for all of the thirty-plus years I've lived in Virginia. The Fourth Musketeer, Vin Sparano, another long-time pal from "Joisey," was laid up at the last minute with the specter of a hip replacement. As we made our way north along I-81, we had plenty of time to ruminate about this special "escape destination" and the gift of being able to share it over the years with best friends. Inevitably, the talk came around to the escapades that make us laugh the hardest:

- Way, way back, George, the fellow who introduced me to this river system, was chugging back to camp after a day's fishing on the lake, when the outboard's propeller hit a submerged log, causing the entire motor to come off the stern of the boat. Luckily (or perhaps not, depending on your perspective), George was holding onto the motor's handle at the time. As his fishing partner that day likes to tell it, the motor kept running, even though totally submerged—as was George's right arm right up to the shoulder—and George was vibrating to the rhythm of the thrashing prop until he somehow managed to hit the cutoff switch.
- During another visit years back, when we still had lots of youthful energy and little sense, we hit a long spell of lousy weather at the McFarlane Camp, as we called it. After a couple days of rain, we were largely reduced to having a game of "baseball" using a fallen, bat-length tree branch and a pile of overripe cabbages that we found in the camp dump. When the cabbages ran out, we pitched old carrots and finally rocks and such. Then the beer came out, stirring our creative juices. After a while we decided to research what would happen if a small propane tank about the size of a large roll of hamburger meat were tied to a suitable piece of wood and floated out into

the wide spot in the river in front of camp, then "propelled" with the help of a .22 rifle. Best thing that happened after that was it started raining again.

- One day we were working a large pool on the river upstream of the camp. The bass were hitting that morning, and we were fired up. Fred, fishing from a boat, was casting his favorite lure, a silver spoon, to a shoreline boulder where the water dropped off dramatically. As the boat drifted farther from the boulder, he muscled out a long cast and said a bad word or two when the spoon caught on an overhanging branch of a large shoreside tree. In an effort to free the lure, he reared back on his rod—hard enough to break the line. Too high to manipulate from the boat and well out from shore, the lure shimmered tantalizingly in the sun. Though fishing from shore, I could see the glint of determination in my bud's eyes as he turned the boat downstream and took off.

"Where you going?" I yelled over the motor's roar.

"Back to camp to get an ax!" was the shouted reply.

What? The guy was going to cut down the tree to salvage his lure! Sure enough, some minutes later the boat returned, and Fred hopped out with an ancient double-bitted ax and strode up to the offending tree. Lifting the ax, he gave the trunk his best shot. As we all watched, the lure shuddered a bit—and fell into dark water probably fifteen to twenty feet deep! End of story. But not end of laughter, which continues to this day.

Trout in Paradise

An alpine world dotted with jewel-like lakes full of cutthroat and rainbow trout that willingly strike almost any fly pattern or small spinner. Sound like paradise? The place I have in mind is indeed the stuff of angling dreams, but getting there can exact a price.

Last summer I spent ten days roaming around on horseback in the Frank Church/River of No Return Wilderness in central Idaho, part of a six-person Trail Riders of the Wilderness group sponsored by the conservation organization American Forests. Headquartering at the Salmon River Lodge, we rode out of a high-country camp just about every day to explore and fish a different lake, each set in a magnificent glacial cirque and seemingly more beautiful than the one we'd seen the previous day. Not one of them failed to yield colorful, healthy cutts or rainbows up to sixteen inches in length.

The fishing here is mostly in lakes, though there are a few streams chock full of pan-size trout. During our stay, forest fires spawned by the dry summer restricted our travel somewhat, and we didn't get to try the streams. But no matter—Basin, Black, Upper and Lower Cottonwood, and other incredibly clear lakes easily yielded their trout riches to the delicate drop of a dry fly or the flash of a spinner.

The closest fire was twelve miles away—nothing to worry much about, the outfitter told us. There was no wind to speak of, and the two fires were moving slowly, parallel to the route we would follow, up out of the Salmon River Gorge and into the subalpine high country of the RNR Wilderness.

I wasn't much worried. But I was smoldering a little. This ten-day August packtrip had been the light at the end of my tunnel for the better part of a year—no, come to think of it, for most of my lifetime. Being brought up in New Jersey doesn't give an outdoors-minded kid much exposure to wild country. Neither do desk jobs in places like New York City and Washington, DC. But such places fuel a man's fire to get up high where the air is clean and cold and the sky is cobalt blue by day and star-pulsing black velvet by night.

That remote country on the rooftop of the Rockies has far more than trout to entertain and enrich the visitor. It is a place of eagles and elk, mountain sheep and goats, superb vistas and solitude. We saw not another soul during our entire stay there.

The area's remoteness is part of both its charm and its challenge. There's only one way into the part of the wilderness we visited— other than rafting down the whitewater Salmon River or chartering a small plane to fly into a tiny airstrip in the high country. You drive west from the hamlet of North Fork, Idaho, some forty-five miles, most of it gravel or dirt, to road's end in the Salmon River Gorge, second deepest in the U.S. There, you have two choices: Head up into the alpine zone on your own (and if you do this, plan carefully, for that rugged up-and-down country is not forgiving of mistakes or forgotten gear) or hire an outfitter to take care of the trip details.

Our group was provided saddle and pack horses, camping gear, and a five-person crew to feed us and wrangle horses—for a total fee of $85 a day per person. The price included a night on each end of the trip at the Salmon River Lodge, across the river from road's end.

These folks, incidentally, are the only outfitters licensed to operate in that part of the River of No Return Wilderness. They can also provide spot-pack trips in the high country, and other options including trips that combine high-lakes fishing with rafting or jetboating on the Salmon River.

The Fish-and-People Name Game

As I swam up out of a deep sleep this morning, other things swam up with me. No, it wasn't a nightmare. It was images of various fish, and they were somehow juxtaposed with people I've known or known about who have names reflecting creatures of the deep (or shallow, as the case may be).

No, this weird "daymare" wasn't brought on by the one glass of Irish whiskey I'd sipped before dinner last evening. I suppose it was a result of certain facts of my life: I've been a fisherman since my Dad took me down to the local lake for the first time at age six—freshwater and salt, rivers, lakes, and oceans, coast to coast and from Canada to Cozumel. And I toiled on the editorial staff of a national fishing magazine for fifteen years and have written about fishing for outlets ranging from *Sports Afield* to airline mags to the *New York Times*.

I suppose such a strange conjuring was inevitable. After all, for several years during my tenure at *Outdoor Life*, my boss, the managing editor and later editor, was named Chet Fish. I am not making this up! Chet was a fine guy and a darned good editor, but not much of a fisherman.

Back then, *Outdoor Life* was owned by a small publishing firm that also held *Popular Science* mag. When that company was bought by Times Mirror Publishing out of California, they brought in a man to "oversee" the well-meshing workings of our editorial staff. The guy's surname was Fry—"fry" being a word for the young of many fish species. Shortly thereafter, I moved on downstream.

Then there's Marilyn "Guppy" Blair, a veterinarian at the Idaho Fish Health Center, one of nine such places run by the U.S. Fish and Wildlife Service (USFWS). Located at the Dworshak National Fish Hatchery in that state's southern panhandle, the Center serves as a kind of regional medical facility for fish in the Northwest. Guppy monitors the general health of hatchery fish, screens them for dangerous pathogens, and recommends and provides treatments for specific fish diseases.

Guppy earned her nickname while on her high-school track team, where she followed in the footsteps of her older sister—who had been dubbed Fishy.

Oh, yes—Guppy's maiden name was Fishback. I kid you not!

"What can I say," she quips. "I started with a fishy name and ended up with a fishy job."

It continues: Wrasses are a diverse family of about 500 fish species, most of them saltwater varieties inhabiting the Pacific, Atlantic, and Indian oceans. Other Wrasses are a land-dwelling family who raised a boy named Colby, who eventually became a biologist at the Columbia Fish and Wildlife Conservation Office in Missouri.

No, he doesn't work with wrasses—I suppose that would be carrying this random thing a bit too far into the cther. Currently (note the double-entendre hint here about water flow, or current? Sorry 'bout that), Colby is working with the federally endangered pallid sturgeon and shallow-water habitat creation on the Missouri River.

Point of interest: The pallid sturgeon, called the "dinosaur of the Missouri River," has a long, flat snout, several rows of bony "scutes" or plates, and the potential to reach seven feet in length. It struggles to survive in a world vastly altered by dams and reservoirs.

Mr. Wrasse has never met his underwater namesake.

Can you handle more? OK, five species of gar, a long, toothy, primitive creature, swim in North American waters. Antediluvian in appearance, gars can breathe air if they need to. Gar Holmes, on the other hand, is a scaleless, hairy, bipedal human who lives in northwest Montana and cannot "breathe" water. Of course, he works with fish, at Creston National Fish Hatchery there. Among his charges are west-slope cutthroat trout, rainbow trout, and the threatened bull trout.

It's possible that Gar could meet gar head-on: Two of the USFWS's hatcheries, Tishomingo in Oklahoma and Private John Allen in Mississippi, have been working to study, monitor, and even spawn alligator gar, which have suffered from widespread habitat destruction. This big-river fish can attain a weight of more than 300 pounds—not even the hulking, hairy Gar has been able to do that!

Mercifully, I'm almost done. There's Kevin Blueback (who shares his surname with a herring); Kevin stocks salmon in Oregon. And Vicki and John Finn, who study salmon. Vina Frye works with— you guessed it—fish fry. Anglin and Fishler share office space at a hatchery.

Whew! I'm going back to sleep.

Uncle Homer with a hulking largemouth bass.

Uncle Homer: A Trophy in the Flesh
By Glen Lau

A few years ago, the fishing community across the nation mourned the death of its favorite uncle—Homer Circle, who died unexpectedly in June 2012 in Ocala, Florida at the age of ninety-seven. His monthly column in *Bassmaster* magazine, "Ask Uncle Homer," was one of the most popular, prolific, and influential in the history of bass fishing. He wrote—and fished—actively until his death.

He was perhaps best known as the long-time fishing editor for *Sports Afield* magazine, serving in that role from 1968 through 2002. He was the author of numerous books, including *The Art of Plug Fishing* (1965), *New Guide to Bass Fishing* (1972), *Worming and Plugging for Bass* (1972), *Circle on Bass* (1996), and *Bass Wisdom* (2000). He hosted a variety of TV fishing programs and starred in two films, "Bigmouth" in 1973 and "Bigmouth Forever" in 1996.

Born in Springfield, Ohio in 1914, Circle began his writing career for his hometown newspaper, then went to work for Heddon Lures, rising to vice president of the company. In the 1960s he moved to central Florida because it gave him the opportunity to bass-fish all year. A former president of the Outdoor Writers Association of America, he received countless awards, including induction into the Fresh Water Fishing Hall of Fame in 2007. In 1996 he was the recipient of the American Sportfishing Association Lifetime Achievement Award.

He and his wife Gayle had been married for seventy years by the time she died in 2007. This writer was blessed to develop a close friendship with Homer that lasted until his death. We fished together weekly, weather permitting, with Homer parked in the bow of my johnboat and I positioning the craft to give my friend the first and best cast at likely targets.

Our last trip was just five days before he died. We fished from 2 to 5 p.m., and he caught six and I caught five—just the way I liked it. There isn't anybody like him. He touched the lives of thousands and thousands of people and was often called on to pray during banquets for the Bassmaster Classic and many other gatherings. His prayer, left, like Homer, is part of the fabric of the sport we love so much.

The Fisherman's Prayer

God grant that I may live to fish
until my dying day;
And when it comes to my last cast,
I'll then most humbly pray;
When in the Lord's safe landing net
I lie in final sleep;
That in His mercy I'll be judged
as good enough to keep.

Homer Circle

Text and poem reprinted with permission of the author.

Brian's World

A very small person is living in our home these days. He showed up last April 20, weighing in at nine pounds fourteen ounces—a fact his mother will never forget. His most prominent features are his chipmunk cheeks and deep blue eyes. His ready smile and total trust make it impossible for his parents and sister and brother to keep their hands off him.

But the joy of Brian is mingled with uneasiness about the world he'll be growing up in. His world will be largely determined by our generation—a sobering and even frightening thought to anyone who read the paper this morning. His very presence is adding already to the mounting pressures being exerted on the natural resources of this nation. So when I look at him, I can't help but think that it's my responsibility, and yours, to see to it that his world will be a fit place to live.

Maybe it's wishful thinking, but here's what I hope Brian's world will be like:

It will be a place where men and women once again try to live by a code of morality and ethics, where people need no longer view politicians as self-serving, religious leaders as hypocrites, lawyers as shysters, and bankers and businessmen as something less than honest.

It will be a place where TV and other media begin to live up to their enormous responsibility to elevate and educate, as well as to inform and entertain, and allow the limitless goodness and positiveness of people to at least share the front pages and the prime-time newscasts with the rapes and finagling and world unrest and other negatives with which our generation is constantly bombarded, and which by themselves breed more of the same.

It will be a place where conservation of our natural resources is a way of life rather than a word that starts an argument or is used as a crutch. This nation, I pray, will have lost by then its reputation as the most wasteful society of all time and be on the road to becoming a truly conserving society that husbands its resources wisely.

Brian's world will be a place where the "me-first" mentality that afflicts our generation like a creeping cancer is somehow miraculously metamorphosed into conscious caring for the other guy. No longer will the nation's insatiable demand for luxuries and shallow diversions gobble up raw materials at a mindless pace and deprive others here and around the world—those who can least bear it—of the very essentials of life and sanity.

Yes, maybe I'm jousting with windmills. Maybe that's far too much even to hope for in the span of just one generation.

But I believe in the innate goodness of mankind, and I'm unwilling to accept the idea that Brian's world will be about the same as ours. I simply can't accept the thought that our legacy to him and his generation will be rivers so polluted that they catch fire, dead lakes, fish made inedible by mercury, wildlife habitat devastated by massive clearcuts or unrelieved carpets of concrete, or regal redwoods senselessly vandalized in order to make a "point." And I hope my son will be wise enough to realize that our forests and other renewable resources are meant to be used for the betterment of the human condition. Used to create homes, paper, and other products, used for recreation and peace of mind, used to hold the soil and break the wind.

I hope he'll know that the natural world is a mirror of his own future. Use it wisely and well, Brian—because if you consume too much or put too much off-limits to people, you will impoverish your own son's future.—**Editorial,** *American Forests* **magazine, September 1978**

Letter to a New Daughter

DEAR KRISTIN:

You made an unforgettable debut last night, you know. When your Mom and I held you for the first time—all nine pounds, four ounces of you—listened to your initial comment on life, and watched your tiny, beautifully formed fingers begin to sense your newfound freedom, we were immediately and irrevocable smitten.

We bid you welcome, our fourth and final child, and we want you to know—as soon as you are old enough to read and understand this letter—that we will do everything in our power to make your life rich, fulfilling, and joy-filled.

We have some gifts for you, gifts we hope you will receive at just the right times as the hours of your days and the days of your years open before you to reveal them. Some of them you already have. Some of them we can promise to give you, or help you to give to yourself. Others we can only wish for you; if you truly seek them, they will be yours as surely as the human spirit can attain goals that the world will tell you are not possible.

We give you the sky. Get up early to watch a porcelain moon glide below a brightening horizon; look closely at the burnished sentinels of day's end. You will learn about time, and eternity, and yourself.

We give you all the other elements of the natural world. This gift comes in the most colorful and magnificent wrappings you'll ever see, and there are so many things you can do with it. A man named Henry Turner Bailey has described this gift very well:

"All children should have the vision of dew-drenched mornings flashing with priceless gems; of grainfields and woodlands yielding to the feet of the wind. They should feel the joy of seed time and harvest, of dazzling summer noons, and of creaking, glittering winter nights.

"They should experience the thrill of being out in the rain without umbrellas or rubber coats or buckled overshoes; of riding a white birch, of sliding down pine boughs, of climbing ledges and tall trees, of leaping into a transparent pool.

"They ought to know the smell of wet earth; of new-mown hay. Of blossoming wild grape and honeysuckle, of an apple orchard in May and of a pine forest in July; the crushed leaves of wax myrtle, sweet fern, mint, and fir; of the breath of cattle and of fog blown inland from the sea.

"They should hear the answer the trees make to the rain and the wind; the sound of rippling and falling water; the muffled roar of the sea in a storm. They should know the sound of bees in a plum tree in May, of frogs in a bog in April, of crickets in the dark in September. They should hear a leafless ash hum, an old tree groan, and the incomparable music of floating ice tinkling along beneath the frozen crystal roof of some flooded glade.

"They should have a chance to chase butterflies and catch fish, to ride on a load of hay, to cook over an open fire, to tramp new country, to sleep under the open sky. They should have the thrill of discovering that Nature will honor the humblest seed they plant."

Take pleasure in our natural world, Kristin. Learn from it, and find hope in it. Someday—maybe as you stand in the flame of the autumn woods—you'll hear its timeless message of life lost and life renewed, life to be used wisely for the benefit of us all.

We give you one final gift. It can be found in the good example of your older sister and brothers, and in the eyes of your grandparents, who are certain to spoil you and teach you with the gentleness and wisdom of their years. You could have seen it in the circle of friends who kept a vigil in a tiny room at the hospital, waiting for your arrival. And we suspect that you will find it someday in the eyes of some winsome young man who will come to take you away. It is the ultimate gift—the essence of happiness. It is the gift of people who will love you for yourself, whatever you are and despite what you are not.

Welcome to our world!—**Editorial,** *American Forests* **magazine, January 1981**

Chapter 3

The Cast

O ne inky night, a friend and I cast surface plugs from an ancient wooden rowboat toward the dimly made out shore of an Ontario lake. Our target: chunky smallmouth bass emboldened by the darkness to feed in the shallows. My friend's Jitterbug was burbling back toward us when something a whole lot bigger than a bass engulfed it in a boil the size of a Cadillac's hood. He set the hook, and the unseen hulk shot away, making the reel scream like the heroine in a horror movie. Then suddenly the line went slack. Thinking he'd lost the big fish, my buddy was reeling in nonchalantly when something that looked as big as an oar against the starry sky launched into the air no more than five feet from the boat, shook its head the way a wet Labrador gets rid of water, broke or bit through the line, and bellyflopped back into its element, showering us in the process.

My crony, his knees beating a tattoo on the sides of the old boat, looked my way and said, "Dunno if I want to cast out *there* again."

That critter was probably a big muskellunge with needle-like teeth a half-inch long. I'm sure my friend didn't think of it this way, but isn't there something spiritual, something *trusting,* about tying to a wispy strand of plastic a concoction of metal and balsa resembling nothing that ever lived on or near water—your intent being to fool a creature with a brain the size of a pea? You cast your lure upon the water, knowing that your chances for success are maybe one in fifty under most conditions, and when the fish aren't biting, each subsequent cast becomes a longer leap of faith.

Sometimes, talking to God—some folks call it praying—is like that. I seem always to be asking Him for something—a raise, a big fish, direction for a teenager—and often my pleas seem to land in fishless water. But the more I ask, the better I feel. Because more often than not, eventually I hook my answer. Maybe it's a flat "NO!" or "Perhaps later" or "This is not what you need right now—try another way."

Fishing can help you to believe—and to listen for answers.

Fish Dog

Total focus. Barely suppressed desire. Avarice! The Lab's face mirrored all of those as he stood in shallow water next to me, rich brown eyes riveted on the little red-and-white fishing bobber that had suddenly bounced twice and then streaked away toward a mostly submerged tree limb. Labradors are retrievers, not pointing dogs, but this one was exhibiting a classic point, head rigid and extended bob-berward, hindquarters quivering with excitement.

"Sam–you STAY!" I said in my sternest dog-training voice.

The bobber plunged beneath the surface, and Sam took two steps out into the lake. It didn't faze him that the water was now lapping at his lower jaw, though he did raise his head just a tad. It also didn't faze him that I was in over my low boots and doing the Spastic Chicken as I raised the light spinning rod with the left hand while grabbing for his collar with the right. Now I had a hand-sized bluegill thrashing on the surface a yard in front of an ardent, black, ninety-five-pound, fish-eating Creature from Hell. Film at 11.

Sam came into our lives much smaller but no less animated seven years ago, a gift for daughter Kristin's eleventh birthday. Since then he has wormed (pun intended) his way into our family's affections like no other pet we've ever had. Never before has Dear Spouse allowed an animal to live inside our walls, especially one whose black coat mostly ends up on our white kitchen floor during all the months lacking an "r."

When he shamelessly parks his sizable derriere in Krissie's lap and looks up at one of us with his big slobbery smile, there's no way not to love him—even if he has just put a Labrador-size hole in our porch screen door in his desire to dispatch the resident groundhog that makes sure our garden doesn't overproduce.

Note fish tail in Sam's maw.
All our Labs are named Sam.

But it's Sam's piscatorial proclivity that endears him most to me. Since his puppyhood, I have taken him along on trout-fishing forays in Virginia's Blue Ridge. It was fascinating to watch him gradually tire of chasing birds and sniffing old deer tracks and begin to shadow me as I fished. Today he is truly my fishing sidekick. He stands next to me as I wade, swimming when he has to, whether the water is snowmelt frigid or summer tepid, his gaze as focused as mine on the place where the line enters the water. When I hook a fish, he gets all quivery and bug-eyed, but nowadays he's usually able to restrain his retrieving instincts and let me land the trout.

Sam doesn't need much incentive to keep him interested. But occasionally I'll catch a small chub or sucker and toss it to him. Sometimes he gulps it down. But now and then he'll walk up and down the bank for a while with the fish in his mouth headfirst, its tail flicking up and down just beyond his muzzle, looking for all the world like some demented black serpent.

Sam is the kind of dog that comes into a family's life just once, if they are very lucky. Now, if I could just train him to clean my catch....

The Smartest Fish in America

Care to match wits with a creature whose brain is smaller than its eggs? Here's how to find the think tanks of the piscatorial world.

It's disheartening to face up to the undeniable realization that you're dumber than a perch. But there it was: We were in a fishing camp in the backwoods of Ontario. We had pretty much exhausted the contents of our coolers, and the glamorpusses of the gamefish world had gone on an extended hunger strike. We would eat no delectable walleyes, no white-fleshed smallmouth bass, not even any bony northern pike this night.

But no problem—the lake and its feeder river are loaded with yellow perch. All you do is impale an earthworm on a small hook, put a bobber four feet up the line, and chuck the whole shebang out next to a line of lily pads. In addition to being very good to eat, perch are piscatorial nuckledraggers. They'll take a live worm anytime, anywhere.

Later, as my cronies and I ate our dinner of peanut butter, hot peppers, and beer, we had time to reflect on the intellectual prowess of the human species *vis à vis* that of various members of the waterbound legions. We humans attribute the trait of intelligence to some of them by simple virtue of their elegant good looks (the rainbow trout, the dolphinfish), their regal bearing (the king salmon, the muskellunge), or their spirit-lifting home waters (the arctic char, the striped marlin). But smarts among fish are in the eyes of the rod holder, and are likely to be largely dependent on how many times he or she has been skunked by a given species.

The following slate of nominees for Smartest Gamefish is not presented in any order of worthiness. Instead, they are species that have scored straight "A"s with me and with a few fishing partners who can claim some pretty fair scholastic achievements themselves.

ATLANTIC SALMON

No less an authority than Izaak Walton himself called this silvery, leaping creature "king amongst gamefish." Along with its West

Coast cousin the king salmon, the Atlantic salmon is potentially the largest gamefish you can catch in fresh water. After spending most of its life trying to survive the many perils of the sea, *Salmo salar* returns unerringly to the river of its birth, where it offers perhaps the supreme sportfishing challenge.

Wherever he is found, except in a few Canadian rivers, you must seek this fish with a fly rod—a wispy seven- to ten-foot concoction of graphite or boron that delivers either a dry (floating) or wet (sinking) fly upwards of seventy feet to where you think a fish may lie in the current. Much has been made of the esoterica of flycasting, but it really isn't all that difficult—for a smart fisherman, that is.

The salmon, on the other hand, can seem maddeningly intelligent as they ignore cast after cast. But when salmon enter a river, they do not seek food. When they do strike, it's apparently out of "annoyance" or memory of a food they inhaled during the time spent in the river after birth and before heading to sea. The smart fisherman must keep casting repetitively until a fly of the right size and shape, worked at just the correct depth and speed, is sucked in by a salmon.

SMALLMOUTH BASS

The "smallie," aka bronzeback, is a close friend of mine, and if you get up close and personal with him, he'll treat you to some of the best angling days you'll ever have. Not as widely distributed as his blood brother the largemouth, he prefers cool, clean, swift rivers and deep, clear, rocky lakes. He'll take a wide variety of lures, flies, and natural baits, and watching him blast a surface lure under a flaming Canadian sunset is nirvana for this writer.

And I'm not alone. Listen to Jack Lorenz, for many years the chief executive of the Izaak Walton League of America:

"In June, Chequamegon Bay on Lake Superior near Ashland, Wisconsin, is crawling with big post-spawn bronzebacks. One day's action still reminds me of an auto demolition derby at a county fair. For more than eight hours, two- to five-pound fish homed in on my lures as if they were their last meal and crushed them at top speed. The second they felt the barb, those golden-brown bruisers shot skyward like missiles from a Polaris sub and proceeded to do the funky chicken across the surface in an effort to throw the hook. They often succeeded.

"Only smallmouths give me that sort of tussle. If power, tenacity, and acrobatics are indicators of a fish's intellectual capacity, the smallmouth has to be world-class in the smarts department."

BONEFISH

You're wading a sparkling, knee-deep sand flat in the Keys, or Andros Island in the Bahamas, or the Yucatan coast of Mexico. Armed with a fly rod or light spinning rod and good sunglasses, you seek the telltale surface disturbance caused by the tail of a bonefish whose business end is nuzzling the bottom for some edible morsel. You spot one against the sun-dappled sand, tremble, watch its line of progress, and drop fly or bait in its path. Your heart's in your throat as the sleek, silvery creature with the underslung lower jaw pounces on your offering. You raise the rod, and the fight of your life begins as the fish bolts away in a contrail of bubbles and your reel screams like a banshee.

Few people know the bonefish as intimately as Rich Stanczyk, whose family has operated Bud and Mary's Marina and guide service at Islamorada on the Florida Keys for half a century. I asked Stanczyk, who has guided the likes of Ted Williams, Dan Marino, and Paul Newman, whether he thought the bonefish was a bonafide whiz kid among fishes.

"Well, they're just so strong, and their senses are so keen. I pole my clients along the flats in a shallow-draft boat with a casting platform, and any sound—the scrape of a shoe on the deck, the click of my pole against a shell on the bottom—is enough to send a tailing bone streaking away. Are they smart? I usually guide very experienced anglers, and I almost always bet two bucks on the bonefish."

MUSKELLUNGE

This torpedo-shaped water wolf is either consummately wary or he eats like a big snake—very seldom but very well. It's probably a combination of both factors, but knowledgeable anglers generally

71

Where Smart People Fish for Smart Fish

Atlantic Salmon: Try the Grand Cascapedia, Matapedia, Tetagouche, and Restigouche rivers on Canada's Gaspé Peninsula; the Moisie on Quebec's north shore of the Gulf of St. Lawrence; some of the small rivers on mostly government-operated Anticosti Island in the Gulf; and the Miramichi in New Brunswick.

Smallmouth Bass: James River, north and south forks of the Shenandoah, and the New River in Virginia; Pennsylvania's Susquehanna River; Lake Champlain in New York and Vermont; Maine's Cheputnicook Lakes and Grand Lake Stream areas and Penobscot and Androscoggin Rivers; and the Boundary Waters Canoe Area on the Minnesota/Ontario border.

Bonefish: The Florida Keys; almost anywhere in the Bahamas (Long Island, Great Exuma, Great Abaco, Berry Islands, Eleuthera, and Andros Islands); Mexico's Yucatan Peninsula, including Cozumel.

Muskellunge: The Turtle-Flambeau Flowage and other lakes in Wisconsin's Hayward area; Wabigoon and other Ontario lakes north of International Falls, Minnesota; many spots in the St. Lawrence River, including where it flows out of Lake Ontario; the Juniata River in Pennsylvania.

Striped Bass: Montauk, New York; Outer Cape Cod and Cuttyhunk, Massachusetts; Sandy Hook to Barnegat Bay, New Jersey; Chesapeake Bay in Maryland and Virginia; Russian River, California; Umpqua River, Oregon.

agree that it takes an average of five full days of fishing or 2,000 casts to get a solid strike from a respectable muskie.

Guess I'm the exception to the rule. Some 800 years ago, when I was young, one of my first dozen casts into a muskie river in southern Ontario brought a strike that I could feel up into my shoulders. For the next twenty minutes, something—beaver? submarine? nah, it had to be a muskellunge—towed two of us in a steel boat that must have weighed 500 pounds up and down that section of river until the snap swivel broke. That fish will live in my mind's eye as long I'm around.

The muskie is moody, unpredictable, and possessed of very large teeth that have caused my blood to drip on boats from Ontario to Minnesota. Is he smart? I think so.

STRIPED BASS

This silvery denizen of both sea and sweetwater has long been known among angling literati as the rather plump dude in the pin-striped suit—kind of suave and knowing. But since fishermen found out—just a

Biggest of the Smartest

SPECIES	WEIGHT	WHERE CAUGHT	DATE	ANGLER
Smallmouth bass	11 lb. 15 oz.	Dale Hollow Res., TN	4/24/69	John Gorman
Striped bass	81 lb. 14 oz.	Long Island Sound, CT	8/9/11	Gregory Myerson
Striped bass (landlocked)	69 lb. 9 oz.	Black Warrior R., AL	2/28/13	James Bramlett
Bonefish	16 lb.	Bimini, Bahamas	2/25/71	Jerry Lavenstein
Muskellunge	67 lb. 8 oz.	Lake Court Oreilles, WI	7/24/49	Cal Johnson
Salmon, Atlantic	79 lb. 2 oz.	Tana River, Norway	1/1/28	Henrik Henriksen

Source: International Game Fish Association

few decades ago—that he is a sucker for large flies, he is gaining a reputation as being dumb as dirt. Here's the word according to Vin T. Sparano, who was on the editorial staff of *Outdoor Life* for an incredible fifty-four years, the last five as Editor-in-Chief:

"Fly fishing for stripers off the northeast coast, centering around Barnegat Bay, New Jersey, where I live, can be spectacular. From October 1 to Christmas especially, stripers will hit all day long in and near the surf. A boat really puts you in the catbird seat. Watch the seabirds for telltale signs of feeding fish, and you can catch stripers until your arms give out. Last fall, as a stunt, I hooked two bass with two flyrods at the same time. What did I prove? That I'm not as dexterous as I used to be!"

Lures of the Luminaries

What do bigshots dream about when fishing is their thing? What eggs them on is the same thing they use to attract fish.

What do you suppose a guy like, say, the President thinks about—maybe even *yearns* for—when he finds a moment free of the press of momentous decisions? What dances through the mind of H. Norman Schwarzkopf now that he's doing TV spots rather than blasting across some God-forsaken desert in the bowels of an armored personnel carrier? What drives the dreams of golfing great Curtis Strange now that he's done lifting U.S. Open Championship trophies for photo ops?

These and others of the nation's notables, I've discovered, aren't all that much different from you and me. However weighty their pursuits, however demanding or glamorous their lives as luminaries may be, give them a moment to think about flexing a fishing rod on stream or pond or lake or ocean, and something lights up inside.

Each of the people interviewed for this article is an angler down where it counts. Each of them was gracious enough to share an insight into the making of a fisherman. Most of those insights revolve around a particular artificial or natural lure or bait—fly, plug, worm, spinner, whatever—that stimulated a lifelong interest in fishing.

Every fisherman, famous or not, can conjure up a lure that transcends the tacklebox and is elevated in our mind's eye to icon status. So real to me that it almost pulses in memory is a Mickey Finn streamer that brought a six-pound landlocked salmon soaring up out of Quebec's Kaniapiscau River.

But enough about us common folk. We thought it might be a hoot to ask some household names about their lures of a lifetime. Here are the results:

George H. W. Bush
Former President of the United States

I've had a lifelong love for the outdoors. I'll never be one of the world's best fishermen, but I'm one of the most enthusiastic.

I've fished from coast to coast and in several of our national parks, but over the past few years my more frequent outings have been to the Florida Keys for bonefishing, down to Alabama for a little bass fishing, and up on the coast of Maine to tangle with blue-fish and stripers.

I use many makes and types of fishing tackle, including a few homemade lures created by my fishing friend, "Tackle Master" Bob Boilard. Bob will use old kitchen spoons, odd feathers, and even the hair of a child's halloween mask in his lures. He makes some great topwater poppers. The ones I like resemble pogies, which when frightened jump to the surface and attract blues. It's such a thrill to see a husky bluefish explode on your lure.

For blues I like light-duty spinning and baitcasting outfits and ten- to fourteen-pound-test lines. Some say ten-pound-test is too light for twelve-pound bluefish, but I like it. You need a wire leader, though. I release most of the fish I catch, but on occasion I'll bring a few blues home for dinner—same for the mackerel that run in enormous schools along the northeast coast in early summer.

Wherever I fish and for whatever species, it's a pleasure just being out there. The outdoors clears the mind and is good for the soul.

Let me end with a little anecdote about my "lure of a lifetime." This may not be what readers might expect, but the family kind of enjoys talking about it. It happened on our boat *Fidelity* off Walker's Point in Maine.

I was just sitting in the boat as my son Jeb started casting. Well, he hooked something right away—his dad. One of the hooks went right through my earlobe. A Secret Service agent used wire cutters to get the hook out, and we went right on fishing. My witness: Canada's then-Prime Minister Brian Mulroney.

I guess you can say I was the "big one" that didn't get away.

H. Norman Schwarzkopf
General, U.S. Army, Retired

It was the summer of 1975. I was a Colonel then, stationed in Alaska. I'd torn an Achilles tendon in an oddball accident and was wearing a walking cast extending to the knee. But the weather was nice, and I had the urge to go fishing.

My family and I headed for a cabin near Homer, but on the way was this gorgeous, pristine lake right along the road. My wife wasn't crazy about dropping me off to fish in my condition, but away she went, and I set up my spinning rod in the slanting glow of evening sunlight.

A handful of fishermen in boats near shore weren't catching anything. I scrounged in my tacklebox for something different, and came up with a strange green and yellow creation shaped like a figure eight. Many years before, I had ordered a box of "a million" mixed lures from a liquidators' catalog, and this lure was among them.

My first cast was about halfway back to me when a Dolly Varden trout of about two pounds smacked that weird lure. The second cast brought a rainbow about the same size. I was hooking something on every cast, and now the guys in the boats were watching me, and working their way in closer.

Pretty soon something a whole lot bigger grabbed the lure. After a long fight, I worked it in close to shore and could see it was a giant rainbow. It still had enough pluck to wrap my line around a snag about six feet from shore. What to do? With my leg cast, I couldn't wade in to free it, and the line was chafing on the snag.

Just then my wife Brenda showed up, and willingly rolled up her jeans as far as they'd go and waded in after that trophy trout. "Try to grab the fish, not the line, "I said. But just as she got within reach, she slipped, grabbed the line, and it snapped. I watched that trout move slowly into the depths carrying my surefire lure—and seeming to gain weight as it went.

That lure blazes in my memory—and I can't even identify it!

Manual Lujan
Former U.S. Secretary of the Interior

I have many, many happy memories of fishing. But I really can't say that I have one old favorite lure. I do, though, always have a lot of *new* favorite lures.

When I was growing up in New Mexico, I often used live bait, like most kids. As my angling experience widened, I began to appreciate plugcasting for bass. Today I favor spinning for bass in rivers like the Shenandoah in Virginia, or working Florida's salt for redfish and sea trout.

My current lure favorites are close to being old standards, I suppose. On rivers I like a classic floating/diving minnow in silver finish, lures like the Rebel and Rapala minnows. In Florida I'll use a deeper-diving lure, one that kicks up a little sand on the bottom. The Bomber-type plugs have always been a lot of fun. I'll work largemouths with a great crankbait called a Poe's Shad.

A lot of fishermen have a warm spot for lures that go back to the early years of this century. But me—I can't wait 'til the new tackle catalogs come out each winter. New discoveries are a big part of fishing for me.

So imagine my delight when I had the chance recently to visit a large national wholesale tackle trade show. What a sight—acres of new rods, reels, and lures. I hope to be out testing potential new personal favorites as you read this.

Jack Elrod

Artist, "Mark Trail" Comic Strip

Many years ago, soon after I started my association with the strip "Mark Trail," the ad agency that handled a well-known outboard motor company wanted to do a bass-fishing movie in the Okefenokee Swamp in south Georgia, using the Mark Trail artists.

The producer had arranged for a park ranger to be our guide, but his area of expertise was the swamp's south end, and our three-boat expedition, with him as our guide, started in from the north end.

The boat trail had been changed by recent rains, and after three hours of motoring and poling through narrow, partly closed channels, the guide realized we were lost. The motors were useless in the thick grass, and poling the heavy boats was impossible. So everyone had to get out into the chest-deep, gator-infested waters and push.

After three more hours, the guide finally located an open trail and we returned to the starting place—without wetting a line.

The only fishing I did that day was from the bank—but it was memorable. I tied on an old wooden spinning-size black-and-white Lazy Ike, and on my first cast, two bass belted the lure at the same time. One of about three pounds was impaled on the lure's rear treble and a one-pounder was solid on the front hooks.

I've never forgotten that day. I still have the lure, and I always try it whenever I get a chance to go fishing.

Curtis Strange
Professional golfer, winner of two U.S. Open Championships

I've got one of the best jobs in the world because I get to do two of the things I love the most—play golf in some of the world's most beautiful settings, and fish nearby—sometimes in the same waters that occasionally attract my fairway shots.

I'm pretty much fixated on largemouth bass, and about eighty percent of the time my lure of choice is a spinnerbait of one kind or another. I just don't seem to have the patience for topwaters or manipulating a minnow imitator or waiting for something to suck in a live bait. I like to chunk it out there and crank it back. Bass don't do much thinking about a spinnerbait—they bang it *now* or leave it alone.

The pro tour takes me to some flat-out wonderful places to fish. On many courses the ponds that golfers fear as hazards are home to real buster bass, and then some. Courses in south Florida and Georgia have Florida-strain largemouths. At Doral in Miami there are ponds holding landlocked tarpon and peacock bass. After the crowds are gone, it's great to be able to partner up with guys like Johnny Miller and Bruce Lietzke and work the club ponds. Quite a few of the tour pros are fishing whackos.

Yes, name puns have always been a part of my life, so maybe you'd like to know about my "strangest" fishing experience. Friends and I were jigging live eels for striped bass in Chesapeake Bay, and were really into them, with fish up to thirty-five pounds. I was rigging up with a new live eel, retying my line to the bottom rig, when the eel slime on my hands and a lurch of the boat caused my favorite jigging rod to slip from my grasp and drop to the bottom of the Bay. I borrowed a replacement, tied on the same eel rig, and some two hours later snagged the lost rod.

Guess that's not too unusual—but it is strange!

Holly Morris
Outdoor writer and editor of the anthologies Uncommon Waters: Women Write about Fishing *and* A Different Angle: Fly Fishing Stories by Women

Recently I was in Cuba filming a TV pilot called "Adventure Divas." Weary after seven long days of interviewing, I steered our roadtrip off course to Lake Zaza, pleading crew respite but secretly desiring a place to wet a line. Flyfishing is my usual method, but I hadn't brought my rod, and I thought, well, "When in Cuba...."

Putting on my best Hemingway swagger and calling up five weeks of intensive Spanish, I ferreted out a man named Charo, who had a boat, a rod, and a pocketful of Cuba's best Romeo y Julieta stogies— but spoke not a word of English. As dawn broke the next day, we motored out for the morning bite. Pink skies. Calm waters. Mimed promises of *pescados grandes*. Though I knew my flyfishing brethren

80

would abhor my near blood-bait fall from grace, I still wasn't prepared for the lure that took the place of my usual tiny nymph: Charo
dangled an eight-inch-long obscenely pink and barbed rubber worm
in front of my face.

The effete flyfisher in me was horrified—but my inner angler,
bred on Midwestern bass and candy-striped Mepps spinners,
screamed out in carnal joy: *These fish must be enormous!* I thought
and started casting.

Even though I don't smoke, I joined Charo in a cigar. We
grudgingly welcomed a boatful of loud Italians into our honey
hole. No sooner had I smoothed out my rusty spincasting than a
hit sent my forearm plunging toward the floorboards. A tank of a
fish, and a fighter in the bargain, the *pescado* I'd hooked was a
largemouth bass that had me waltzing around that tiny boat, Charo
following my lead with net in hand. He seemed nonplussed; but
my endorphins were firing with each and every centimeter of line
that fish took.

I hauled the lunker in and was breathless at its mass. It topped
twelve pounds, dwarfing the measly bass of my suburban Illinois
youth. The vivacious and fishless Italians knocked me out of my
proud stupor with jeers—"*Chiquita Pescado! Chiquita Pescado!*"
(Hot little fisher girl!).

Still, reflecting back on being smack dab in the middle of Cuba,
with not a flyrod, a twirling Mepps, or a shiny spoon in sight, I'd
have to join the Havana Club in extolling the virtues of my new
favorite lure: a long, juicy rubber worm, glistening bright fuscia in
the Caribbean sun.

Flyfishing: Then and Tomorrow

On the scale of human endeavor, figuring out a way to deliver
a bit of fluff and feathers to a dumb fish lying behind a river rock
might seem a kind of Fred Flintstone exercise. Okay, maybe it's not
up there with the discovery of the wheel and the lever, but back in the
second century A.D., Roman author and traveler Claudius Aelianus
was casting across the eons when he penned what is generally con-
sidered the first description of flyfishing. In *de Animalium Natura*,

he told how the locals on the River Astraeus in Macedonia first tried to "match the hatch":

"They fasten red wool round a hook and tie to the wool two wax-colored feathers that grow under a cock's wattles. Then they throw their fly on to the water, and the fish becomes very excited, and comes straight at it." The targets were "fish with speckled skins"—almost certainly brown trout.

Over the years since, countless fisherfolk—this writer included—have found flyfishing to be an irresistible challenge; an elixir for body, mind, and spirit; and a fine reason to set pen to paper and insert film into cameras. Among the most capable chroniclers were Dame Juliana Berners (*Treatyse of Fysshyng Wyth an Angle*, 1496); Izaak Walton (*The Compleat Angler*, 1653); Frederick Halford, Theodore Gordon, Ray Bergman, and Joe Brooks in the nineteenth and early twentieth centuries; and such modern masters as Ernie Schwiebert, Lefty Kreh, and Dave Whitlock.

Despite the passion and eloquence of its devotees, however—or perhaps because of it—flyfishing couldn't seem to shake the cachet of elitism it provoked in casual observers, who viewed it as a sport mainly for those with deep pockets and time on their hands—the Hemingway syndrome. Or they were discouraged by all the special gadgetry and casting skills you needed to do it right. A lot of that misperception was swept away by the 1992 movie *A River Runs Through It*, based on Norman Maclean's wonderful novel. Filmed on the Big Blackfoot and other rivers in Montana, it beautifully evokes the humanity and humor and exquisite art of flyfishing and flycasting. Angler or not, you don't soon forget a scene in which Brad Pitt hooks a monster trout and follows it downstream through deep, boiling water—sans waders.

That movie took flyfishing's fortunes, too, around a bend. The sport's rich-guy reputation has lost its edge, and it is more and more a pursuit for everyman—and everywoman. Along the best drive-to fly waters nowadays, there seems to be an SUV parked every hundred yards and somebody in a rubber suit in every likely run. In headwaters streams in places like Virginia's Shenandoah Park and even Yellowstone, you have to hike a lot farther to get beyond the competition.

Whither goest flyfishing in the new millennium? I posed that question to a trio of the nation's most experienced anglers–Lefty Kreh, author and flycaster extraordinaire (this guy can drop a fly into a saucer at seventy feet using only the tip section of a flyrod); Joe Healy, editor of *Saltwater Fly Fishing* magazine; and Vin Sparano, former editor of *Outdoor Life*. Here's the gist of their wisdom:

People have been experimenting with the long rod in the salt for 100 years, but in the last couple of decades the idea has gone off like a fastball from a major leaguer's bat. It seems odd to see someone with a severely bent flyrod standing braced in the stern of a forty-foot charterboat somewhere in the Gulf Stream when logic tells you he/she ought to be hanging onto a broomstick-stiff trolling rod. One driver in this trend is the recent development of specialized tackle, including tough new rods and clear flylines.

Saltwater aficionadoes are really pushing the envelope in terms of the size of fish taken. Bonefish, permit, and tarpon are still the most popular targets, but these days flyrodders are besting marlin, sharks, and tuna weighing hundreds of pounds.

On its face, this brave new world of flyfishing might not seem especially attractive to women. Think again: Women are flocking to flyfishing in unprecedented numbers, signing up for flycasting schools, signing on at dude ranches and fishing resorts—and setting a bunch of those fishing records as well. Not too long ago, the International Game Fish Association (IGFA) separated the flyfishing records into men's and women's categories, and in the years since, women have established hundreds of new records.

And finally, to the vast credit of today's flyfisherpersons, the great majority release all or most of their catch.

Dinner

One of the first truisms I heard when Dear Spouse and I moved to a small town in central Virginia a few years ago is that the best place to meet and greet just about the entire citizenry of this area is Wal-Mart. Everybody goes there, and if your neighbor happens not to be there on any given day, just go next door and check at Lowe's.

Yep, we buy a good share of our dinner makings over there, but none of that shrink-wrapped stuff can hold a candle to the natural fixin's I bring home from my ramblings in the local streams and puckerbrush. Take the Wednesday before last for example:

At 7 a.m. I could see my breath—just barely, but temps in the mid-fifties made it hard to believe that this was July. Our previous summers here have been hot and stifling from late May on. This was obviously a day to do some rod research on the smallmouth bass and other denizens of the nearby Maury River. A few days' break from the hard rains of the previous couple of months had allowed the river to lose its brown tinge and yet maintain a healthy flow with plenty of white water—perfect conditions.

A few minutes of driving brought me and sidekick Sam, an affable yellow Lab, to one of my favorite stretches. Wade-fishing a local river is just a pure and facile pleasure. To gear up for it, you follow the KISS principle: Keep It Simple, Stupid. I took in hand my little three-ounce ultralight spinning outfit, a pair of cleated wading shoes with a rubber liner to keep my old feet from getting too beat up, and shrugged into a lightweight fishing vest, the pockets of which held all I'd need to entice my quarry.

A twenty-minute morning meander through dappled sunlight and shade took me 'n Sam to a section of river with lots of riffles mixed with deep, fast runs, the kind of habitat where smallies hold and feed. From one of the vest's many pockets came a small plastic lure box containing different color versions of the very best lure I've ever found for this kind of fishing: the Crickhopper. Only a couple of inches long, it looks like a cross between a cricket and a grasshopper. It floats while at rest, but a big downward-pointing lip on the front causes it to dip enticingly when you twitch the rod tip, and swim well under the surface with a tight wiggle when you reel steadily.

With the little yellow lure dangling from the rod tip, I waded in to within casting range of a deep hole dug out by the current below a big boulder. Dropping the lure beyond the rock, I guided it back through the dark little pocket. Whack! Whack! He hit it twice, but managed to avoid the two little treble hooks. No matter: A second cast to the same place brought a solid strike, and the handsome little fish treated me to three jumps free of its element before coming to hand. I unhooked and released the eight-incher, with instructions to send back his Old Man.

There's one little hardship to wading the Maury: The bottom is almost uniformly paved with rocks rounded by the currents. It's like trying to walk on a sea of bowling balls. Sunglasses let you see the bottom more clearly and the boot cleats helped, but my aging feet and ankles bore the brunt of the constant stumbling.

But the rewards were well worth the soreness of my carcass after three and a half hours on the water: I tried to keep track, and by my best estimates I caught some seventy fish that morning, and had a strike on about sixty percent of my casts. If you're not a fisherman, believe me when I tell you that such a success rate is little short of phenomenal.

Now, these weren't fish that posed any danger of pulling me into deep water or anything. Most were six to nine inches long—smallmouths, rock bass, and bluegills. But a few were big enough to "tug on yer rope," as anglers might put it. And thanks to that little light rod, all of them felt like keepers.

And there were a couple of pleasant surprises: In one classic piece of white water, the Crickhopper was intercepted by something that had the rod bent over double. The fish held in the fast water, too big to horse in, and never jumped, so I suspected it wasn't a bronzeback (smallmouth).

I just maintained steady pressure with the little wand, letting the fish take line when he wanted to, and eventually tired him enough to get him close and grab his lower lip. Brightly colored, thirteen-inch rainbow trout! And I hooked two other rainbows not long after that. The fish obviously got into the Maury from the South River, which flows into the Maury and is stocked with trout (the Maury is not, at least not in this area).

Out of another pocket of my vest came a metal stringer, one end of which went through the trout's jaw and the other into a strong loop on my vest. I continued to fish with the trout swimming beside me.

Eventually two decent smallmouths and a hand-size bluegill (a long-ear sunfish, to be totally accurate) joined the trout on the stringer. Dinner!

Needing to give my old dogs (and my old dog) a rest, I left the river, found a log to sit on, shed the waterlogged boots in favor of an old pair of sneaks I'd been toting in the back of the vest, and Sam and I headed for the car. It had been a fine morning.

Chapter 4

SETTING THE HOOK

"Fishing is the only sport where you can watch all your troubles run down a line and get lost in a wonderful creature called a bass." So wrote widely respected angler Homer Circle (you met him earlier in this book), who crafted a fishing column for *Sports Afield* magazine for more years than he cared to remember. "Uncle Homer" was intimately acquainted with fishing's moment of truth—the hook-set.

Much of this sport's allure, he has written, is condensed into those intense seconds when you feel or sense the quarry taking your bait or lure and make the conscious decision to rear back on your rod and send the hook into its jaw. You now have the chance to solve the mystery, to see the creature from that unseen world, know its size and color and fighting ability, watch it leap from that world if you're lucky, and to keep or release it, determining its fate.

But sometimes fisherpeople themselves wind up being the "hookee," so to speak. On my first fishing foray with Dad so many years ago, I was hooked as solidly as any scaly creature I've ever reeled in. And as my knowledge and love of the sport grew, God has held the rod and drawn me to Himself in many ways and places—a Quebec lake with the unlikely name of Mathilde, where one evening my best friend and I were enveloped in a grace-filled moment of utter peace and contentment; along the Chinese Wall in Montana's Bob Marshall Wilderness, where eagles soared and elk bugled and a towering waterfall plunged into my soul; in Alaska's Misty Fiords National Monument, where the immensity and beauty and timelessness of the land filled me with a sureness of a power beyond my wildest imaginings. Where there is grandeur, there is God.

Those and other outdoor high points, however, were just hints, teasers, baits luring my wife Rita and me toward a life-altering experience that impacted our entire family and many of our friends—and has given a whole new definition to the concept of setting the hook:

The Encounter Experience: Fillet of Soul

> **And he said to them, "Follow me, and I**
> **will make you fishers of men."**
> **Immediately they left their nets and followed him.**
> **—Matthew 4:19-20 (NAS)**

It began in 1972. I was well ensconced by then as a member of the editorial staff of *Outdoor Life* magazine—the kind of job I'd dreamed about since my early teenage years. How blessed I was to be able to meld my avocation as an outdoor nut with my vocation as a cog in the big wheel of one of the top three outdoor mags in America. I'd settle in each day in a high-rise office building in midtown Manhattan with a blue pencil (yep, that was a long time ago) and hard copy written by the likes of legends such as Charlie Elliott and Jack O'Connor, Joe Brooks and Ben East. Peering over my shoulder occasionally was Editor Bill Rae, a scowling old Scotsman and a genius in his own right.

The managing editor was a gent named Chet Fish—on my honor, that was his real name—and Chet and I got along well. Soft-spoken, easy-going, and a strong Catholic Christian, he was easy to talk to about work and lots of other topics. One day he mentioned that he and Claire had become involved with an organization called Marriage Encounter, which gathers couples together over a weekend and teaches an unusual method of communication, the goals being to strengthen relationships and promote strong values. He had nothing but good things to say about the group.

Against my "better judgment," I decided to mention our conversation to Rita that night. We'd been married for about ten years, and the honeymoon was definitely over. Our ability and desire to communicate were deteriorating—in fact, we were struggling to hold our marriage together. I was of the opinion that because I worked so hard I had the right to fish, hunt, bowl, play softball—and let her be the prime mover in our family, which at that time included our firstborn, Karen, then eight, and Kevin, six.

That evening and over the next few weeks, Reet and I talked about trying this Marriage Encounter idea. I was luke-warm to spending a whole weekend in a conference room when I could be out whacking the largemouth bass or maybe a tennis ball. But though I was selfish, I don't think I was stupid, and pondering what might happen if we didn't do something to turn our marriage around scared me. And I got to wondering whether the Big Guy just might have something positive in store for us—as He always seems to in our lives.

So we signed up—and the drumbeat began, muted but intriguing, on a Friday evening in July at a retreat house in Princeton, New Jersey. About twenty-five couples gathered in the conference room were given a crash course in the weekend's logistics: A series of talks would be given, each by one of the three presenting couples and the priest who was part of the "team." Following each talk, we listeners would separate, husbands from wives, and write a letter to our spouse, then come back together to "dialogue." The letters, the team explained carefully, were to be centered as much as possible on feelings rather than thoughts.

Warning…Warning!! As soon as I heard that word *feelings*, my male antennae started vibrating. *Am I gonna be stuck in this place for a whole weekend of touchy-feely?* That approach to things was simply not in my mental or emotional makeup. Later, in our room, I told Reet in plain terms how I felt—er, thought—and she asked me to try to suspend my "better judgment" until the next day.

One of the first talks Saturday morning was titled Encounter with Self. *Warning…Warning!!* Forty years before the phrase became popular, I said to Self, *C'mon, Man! Am I about to have my every inner instinct challenged and critiqued and beaten to a pulp?* As I listened to the words of the couple and Fr. Dan, I cringed at many of the points they were sharing about their own struggles and how they had lived their individual lives. But I couldn't help admiring their honesty and their guts, and I also couldn't help looking at my own "masks," the elements of the Bill I strove to project to Reet and to the world, and how those masks influenced my relationship with her and others.

As the weekend progressed, I became increasingly astounded at what was happening to me. I was literally and figuratively being peeled like a Vidalia onion. All my senses seemed to be sharpening. My mind was trying to take in all this new perspective and direction—and not only welcoming it but agreeing with it and reveling in it! It was as if a light had gone on in my soul. But … I simply could not fathom how I had failed to amass this knowledge earlier in my life. I was blessed with the finest pair of parents anybody could ask for—they reflected their love for one another and for God clearly and generously; my five sisters and I knew about unselfish love. Had I just not been paying attention?

An example: one day in my early childhood Mom and Dad were kidding around with one another in the kitchen before he headed off to board a commuter train to New York City. This was back in the days when the milkman delivered quarts of cow juice that had a waxed-paper cap crimped to the top to seal each bottle. She took a new bottle and turned it upside-down above his head. Yep, you guessed it—the cap came loose and Dad and his nice new suit got drenched. Saying not a word, he got up, went upstairs to clean up and change, kissed Mom, and headed off. And yes, he even came home that night!

By Sunday afternoon I was ricocheting off the ceiling fixtures—when I wasn't smiling or crying, that is. At the final gathering, we were asked if we wanted to share a feeling or two. I somehow managed to blubber out something like this: "I simply can't believe what you seven people have done for me and Reet in just two days. This has been the most profound experience of my entire life...."

The final candle on the cake was that the team asked us to consider serving as a presenting couple. Wow! We were flattered, of course, but Reet and I talked it over and decided that, given the long-awaited promotion I'd just been awarded at the office, this wouldn't be the best time for this new challenge, attractive as we both saw it.

Not long after getting home and hugging the kids practically to death, we called my Mom and Dad, knowing they would share our excitement and happiness. That conversation was long and tear-choked but wonderfully encouraging and supportive. Then we collapsed, exhausted physically and emotionally, into bed.

Sometime in the wee hours of the next morning, the phone rang. Mom had suffered a stroke; better come to the hospital. Not long after we'd gathered in a waiting room with Dad and with Pat and Bern and Kathy and Mary Ann and Joan, a nurse came out with the crushing news: we'd lost Mom at the too-young age of sixty-one.

The next few days were a blur, in more ways than one. Never before had Rita and I been battered by so many conflicting emotions:

grief and loss, helplessness and near-depression, all of them magnified by being at the opposite extreme from the soaring joy and confidence and exhilaration of the weekend. But as those days labored by, and at Mom's viewing and burial, we were approached by literally dozens of people we'd never met before. They greeted us with hugs, smiles, caring words, food, and promises of continuing prayer. It was the Marriage Encounter community doing its thing. As this is written in the summer of 2014, forty-two years later, spouse and I can still feel those heartfelt hugs.

In the wake of that emotional hurricane, Reet and I talked a lot more about the possibility that we might help present Encounter weekends. We were still hesitant—neither of us had ever spoken in front of a large audience, there were all those talks to write, and what about the kids—would we be short-changing them? I was right on the edge: Mom would want us to go for it; Dad too. Then the Father of us all reached out with a barely perceptible nudge, and over we went.

A short time later we found ourselves in another conference room with another gang of couples for what was called a Team Training Weekend. We didn't know it then, but the facilitator (bossman) was one Fr. Chuck Gallagher, widely recognized for taking the existing M.E. concept and broadening it to an international level. "Call me Chuck," he told us, flashing his wide and genuine smile above a jutting chin. *Yep, he's Irish,* I whispered to Rita, my uncertainties easing a bit.

It's hard to describe that special time in our lives: words like exhausting, challenging, mind-blowing, and magnificent come to mind. At the risk of coming across as a hard drinker or a pothead, allow me to quote from a letter written to Reet after a talk titled Marriage in God's Plan:

"Right now my deepest feeling is gratitude—leaping, gushing, flooding, crying, smiling, soaring, trembling GRATITUDE! I can feel Him right now in me and in you and in everyone in this room. There is no way I can repay Him for giving me you—you are the vehicle, the catalyst, the medium that helped me truly find Him."

Other talks evoked uneasiness and inadequacies and doubts about whether we would be able to shed our masks and fears and failings and open up to other couples to help them as we had been helped.

Fr. Chuck Gallagher:
Vision and Spunk

"In case you're interested," said the man in the Roman collar to the couples gathered at the end of our Team Training Weekend, "Rooney has some fishing rods and rifles he may be willing to part with." It was his way of saying that my priorities were about to change as Rita and I took on the challenge of helping to give Marriage Encounter weekends in our area. Of course he was wearing his impish, irresistible Irish smile, and I couldn't help but follow suit.

We were soon to learn that our mentor was essentially the father of the Worldwide Marriage Encounter (WWME) movement, developed by Fr. Gabriel Calvo, a Spanish priest, in 1952. In the late 1960s Fr. Chuck adapted the basic premises, and he and some couples began presenting weekends in the New York area. In the early seventies the movement began to expand across the United States and into Canada, Australia, and beyond. The impact of his vision really resonated with couples. Today weekends are presented in almost 100 countries, making it the largest pro-marriage movement in a world that so sorely needs it.

The programs are continually updated to keep abreast of changes in society. WWME now offers evening and half-day programs that are presented at parishes and other church facilities. The weekend program, traditionally set up as an overnight event at a hotel or retreat center, can also be experienced at the parish itself, the couples returning to their homes in the evenings.

Fr. Chuck was eighty-five when he died on July 21, 2013 in New Jersey after a short illness. Our world is better for having had him in our midst.

Worldwide Marriage Encounter offers tools for building and maintaining a strong, Christian marriage in today's world. To learn more, go online to wwme.org, or contact the WWME Office at 909-863-9963.

Interactions with Fr. Chuck were invaluable in showing us the way. And when he made each point, his eyes projected such intensity that we couldn't help but be convinced.

For the next four years we served Marriage Encounter by helping present weekend retreats. I believe we were involved in eighteen, including two in New Orleans. Words simply cannot convey the privilege and fulfillment and joy of watching marriages heal and blossom and glow. That experience—as close to a miracle as I will ever come—invigorated our own marriage, lifted and enriched us in so many ways (including blessing us with a host of fine friends), and led us in new directions.

Our four kids? Karen and Kevin, the two older ones who were on-site during those years, got used to being dragged to strange homes and halls and other places, where they got to make new friends and came to understand a bit better what their crazy parents were up to lately. Brian and Kristin, born after I changed jobs and we moved to Virginia, benefitted from a stable home life and wild stories from their older siblings. Today all are upstanding citizens of whom we are inordinately proud.

I trust that if you, Gentle Reader, have stuck with me this far, you may see the above as a fishing story—but without the exaggerated measurements and the PhotoShop and the wishful imaginings of most angling tales. Never before this experience did I have more than half a clue about fishing's parallels with God's movement in my life. As those four years of active duty with M.E. unfolded, though, there was no way I could deny that Reet and I were being inexorably drawn to the love essence that is God, and in the process learning to draw others in the same direction. If that isn't being "reeled in," I'm fish bait! And when the entity wielding the "rod and reel" is the Big Guy, and sometimes we ourselves, it was, and still is, almost too much to take in.

An aside: OK, I guess calling God the Big Guy could be taken as disrespectful. I see this nickname, though, as a term of endearment, of relationship and friendship and, well, respect. I'm coming to see Him more and more as a fishing buddy, a presence unseen when I'm astream or in a boat but a felt presence nonetheless. This coming fall two longtime buds and I will travel to Ontario for a week of fishing, tall tales, and "friendly rejoinders." I have lots of nicknames for both Jack and Fred, and they for me. Now, some of those could easily be seen as disrespectful (at best). I see them as expressions of love. I think the Big Guy would agree.

Chapter 5

HUNTING FOR GOD

———————•———————

No, I'm not advocating an open season on the Creator of us all (maybe He'll get a laugh out of that one). But to my mind, anyone's chances of sensing, tracking, coming to understand, and finding God soar when he or she wanders in unpeopled country—be it a country lane or a wilderness area. Where the soul soars, there is God. Of course, if you want to follow the advice in Psalm 46 (NAS), "Be still, and know that I am God," you can do so in your bedroom closet or anywhere else. But when you're surrounded by the sounds and scents and sights of the world as He created it, it is so much easier and more delightful to tune in.

And a lot of us do: According to records maintained by state and federal fish and game agencies, in 2013 a total of 27,947,598 people bought fishing licenses and 14,631,327 bought hunting licenses. Hunters pursue animals called game species—deer and elk and moose, wild turkeys (more numerous and widely distributed today in the U.S. than ever before), and a variety of smaller creatures. Most people, especially conservationists, understand that sport hunting is the best overall solution to the problem of keeping populations of these animals within the bounds of what their habitat can support. And the flesh of these wild creatures is generally far healthier fare than what we buy shrink-wrapped in the supermarket.

In Virginia and many other states, hunters get a chance to donate protein to needy families through organizations like Hunters for the Hungry. Last hunting season alone, more than 363,000 pounds of venison was distributed in the Commonwealth through this program. Since H for H was founded in 1991, more than 3.5 million pounds, equal to 13.5 million servings, of venison went to food pantries and other outlets.

But hunting's benefits don't stop there, as witness the stories below in this chapter.

The Squire's Tree

A perch like this can help a hunter take the long view.

The old oak had toppled in a windstorm sometime in the previous six months. It had broken off about ten feet above the ground and fallen uphill—a crotch of three large branches wedging against another mature, still-standing oak. One of those branches extended down to the ground at a shallow angle, inviting a man to walk up it. There, he could sit in comfort and watch a prime piece of acorn woods. At least one deer had found the tree equally comforting; its bed had flattened some of the dead leaves that still clung to the fallen monarch.

I'd found the place a few days earlier, and now, on the opener of Virginia's muzzleloader season, I climbed into my jungle gym well before dawn and sat with my back to the upright oak as a blazing full moon slid westward toward the dark outlines of Virginia's Blue Ridge Mountains. It was a time and place for cosmic thoughts.

My mind conjured up an old house in central New Jersey where Mom and Dad helped my five sisters and me to find out who we were, what love is, and what some of the options were for finding direction in life. As described earlier in this book, my path was ordained for me one day at about age six, when Dad, who loved the natural world, took me fishing for the first time. Something opened up in me that day. It wasn't just the little bobber that began to dance and then plunged out of sight, or those exquisitely unbearable moments before it rose to the surface, no longer attached to the unseen leviathan in the depths. It was the geese overhead and the garter snake in the grass and the somnolent buzzing of insects and the smell of weeds crushed underfoot.

Dad would have appreciated the view from my present perch. He'd have chuckled softly at the thickly plumed red fox that crunched daintily through the moon-rimmed woodlot with a squirrel in its mouth. It hopped up on a dead log that led string-straight to me; at about fifteen feet it looked up at me, widened its eyes, dropped the squirrel, and beat a hasty if relatively dignified retreat.

When the moon dropped behind the ridges, the stars no longer had competition. They pulsed and preened in an ebony sky washed clean by a weather front. After a while, the celestial show in the west began to fade, and I shifted position to sit the opposite way so I could drink in dawn's mauve and blue and yellow and cerise.

It was time to scan the murky woods for the whitetailed deer whose rubs and scrapes were beginning to signal the onset of the rut. Instead, however, I conjured up two gents whose lives had converged with mine in this special place and time. One, the owner of this land—the Squire, in his seventies—was contemplating selling the place and moving closer to his daughter in Florida. The other, Dad, was eighty-nine and, for the first time in his life, in failing health.

Some eloquent man—probably a marketer—said the only constant is change. But as I approach codgerdom myself, the winds of change tend less to fill my sails than to blow me off course. I ride with the guy who said the more things change, the more they remain the same—as witness the following:

I didn't have to clean my muzzleloader after that morning in the Squire's tree. And a month later, on the day after Thanksgiving, we lost my Dad, the gentlest, most caring man I've ever known. Another year has moseyed by since then. The Squire still lives amid his whitetail woods, but the sale is imminent, and I'll soon lose the best hunting land I've ever been privileged to visit.

Six weeks ago, as I perched in full bowhunting camouflage in another area of the Squire's woods, a bobcat appeared at the foot of the ladder stand. The pure essence of stealth, it had materialized without making a sound—which even I would have heard, given the parched leaves of Indian summer. It posed for me—one front foot up on a rock, the other raised and motionless, eyes lasering on a squirrel, and then on me—before moving off as furtive as any leopard.

And just last week as I write this, I sat again up in the Squire's tree—this time paying attention—when a sleek six-point strode purposefully over the top of the hill, toward what appeared to be a hot date. He didn't know it, but his date was with me.

Over the next year, all the summer's green we will eat, my family and I, in the form of prime venison. The fox and the bobcat will continue to wander through my day and night reveries as long as I still dream. And my Dad's kindly ways and love of nature are surely spinning off into tomorrow: "Can we go fishin', Poppop?" is almost always my grandson Grayson's greeting to me.

My son Kevin and I will do everything in our power to nurture Grayson's outdoor leanings. He'll want to follow the dainty whitetail tracks meandering through the acorn woods. He'll come to know how trees grow tall, reproduce, fall, and molder to enrich the earth. And he'll one day sense that humans rooted deep in the soil of life's enduring values need not fear time's erosion of body, spirit, or country.

A Bowhunter's Autumn

**Few moments are as magical as one that reveals
how a lifetime of hunting has carried
you to a special place in your now aging life.**

Gettin' old sucks.

The thought came to me more or less unbidden as I peered up through the gathering gloom at the steps leading up to the too-small platform in the old walnut. That afternoon I'd walked with a forester as he marked some fine mature yellow poplar trees for a selective cut to be made a few months hence. In the process we'd found a fresh antler rub on a cedar five inches across. I couldn't quite make out that whitish mark from the treestand, but it was close enough to make my neck swell at the prospects of what I might see from up there on Virginia's bow-season opener, just a week away now.

I've got sixty-seven autumns on my ledger as I write this, but the sensory delights of that season continue to stir me to the core. Virginia's Blue Ridge serves them up lavishly; russet and gold and bright red illuminate the hollows and hillsides, and the days shorten and the trees shed their clothes and the view lengthens and the antlers grow and the human heart is restless, uncertain, reminded of the dying time but somehow energized by a dimly felt sense of harvest and haven.

Who put the steps on this stand—the beanstalk giant? Last year I had no trouble getting up in the platform; this year I'll have to add at least a couple of rungs, thanks to knees that don't bend like they used to and muscles that have started to whine like a blue-state liberal.

A few weeks earlier I'd dusted off the Mathews Legacy, best bow I've ever hauled back, and cranked it up to my usual sixty pounds of draw weight—immediately discovering that if I wanted to actually hunt with it, I'd have to crank it back down a bit. I did so, and really put a hurtin' on that rubber deer in the back yard. I was ready.

Before first light on the long-anticipated day in the first week of October, I headed up the familiar trail near the foot of Old Rag Mountain. Despite new batteries, the cone of illumination from the Mini-Maglite barely penetrated through the soupy fog to the soggy ground. Smiling at the thought of a slow, drawn-out dawn, I fumbled my way up the stand's now more user-friendly steps and onto the platform, hauled up the Mathews on the line tied to my belt, put on the camo face mask and gloves, and assumed the predator stance.

For a half-hour or so my world was a tiny opening encased in a solid gray womb. Gradually the gray brightened and thinned a bit and I could actually see the ground. Not long thereafter, I thought I heard a sound not unlike antlers scraping on wood. *Uh-huh. Right. And the King of the Woods will be here any minute.* Take it from me: If you wear a hearing aid, you think you hear a lot of things that aren't there, and miss stuff that you really need to hear, like critters crunching leaves.

Alerted now, I very slowly turned my head in the direction of the sound—phantom or not. For fifteen or twenty minutes I neither saw nor heard anything. I'd just begun to cut my eyes back the other way when I caught motion. Soundlessly a sizable animal ghosted through the still-thick mist. For perhaps a minute I couldn't identify it, though it wasn't more than fifteen yards away. It stopped and began to browse—toward me. When it was seven yards from the base of my tree (I later stepped off the distance), it stopped to look around. Antlers! Nice ones, though I couldn't see any details.

It was legal shooting time, and the deer was very close. Moving centimeters at a time, I eased into a directed shooting stance and drew. The buck was oblivious to me, though I thought my thumping heart was surely making the ground shake under me. I released the aluminum shaft, and the buck jumped straight up and then peered around. I hadn't cut a hair.

He moved away from the tree about five yards—and started feeding again! I eased another arrow off the bow quiver, snail-crawled it onto the nocking point (at the little snick, Bubba glanced up, shook his head, and went right back to the chowline), and drew once more. I must have no pride whatsoever if I am willing to put down in print that I missed him again. This time the buck trotted off about twenty yards before stopping to look around. I could barely make him out now, but he stayed nearby for at least another half-hour, during which time I mentally booted myself in the behind, repeatedly shook my head, and couldn't decide whether to cuss or cackle.

You'd think a man who has spent much of his adult life pursuing wild creatures would be able to rein in his excitement at the sight of a whitetail buck with respectable but far from record-book headgear— and I still had no idea how many points the rack carried. Both arrows had passed just over his back, obviously because I hadn't adjusted the aimpoint to compensate for the short range.

As I meandered back to my ops base at the turn-of-the-century farm building, which had housed a few of the people moved out of the mountains when Shenandoah National Park was created in the 1930s, some of the sludge in the back of my mind began oozing toward the front....

Sure, I can glibly say, "When I don't get fired up anymore at the sight of a nice buck, I might as well stay out of the woods." But what happens if the desire and excitement are still there but physical limitations start to overwhelm them?

What happens when I can't get out in the boons anymore?

Will memories and a few mounted heads be enough?

My dad wasn't much of a hunter, but he took on the aging process with great aplomb and dignity right up until he passed at eighty-nine. Hunting and fishing and an insatiable desire to see what's over the next hill are basic elements of who I am. How am I gonna handle it?

Now it is two weeks later. I am back up in the same treestand. The fog is gone; the mental sludge is back in its hole. The smell of the moldering woods and my misting breath in the brisk air of first light are better stimulants than any pothead will ever know.

After a half-hour, two lady deer step demurely along a dim trail within bow range. I mentally wish them a wonderful day and many productive sexual liaisons and watch them move out of sight. Though deer of either sex are legal throughout Virginia's bow season, today I am holding out for a hat rack, or reasonable facsimile thereof.

Two hours later I am beginning to regret that decision. The forest floor is now a mottled montage of shade and bright sunlight. Deer are crepuscular creatures that move about mostly at sunup and sundown, and spend much of midday in their beds. Ah, but it's mid-October and the numerous tree rubs and first ground scrapes speak of the start of the rut, when whitetails get a bit whacky and may strut their stuff at any hour of the day. I hold my position and try to keep my movements to a minimum, though my legs are beginning to protest.

Reprinted with permission of the National Rifle Association.

Instantly I come to full alert: something is moving through a patch of young conifers on a steep slope to my front—a single animal, coming my way. Buck. Nice buck! By the time I can count the nine points on the symmetrical rack, he is down the hill and moving off to my right. I'm afraid he'll pass out of range, but then he makes a sharp right and is heading directly for my tree. I try to make like a glacier while shifting into the required shooting position.

Using just my mouth, I let out what I hope sounds like a buck grunt but reminds me more of intestinal gas, and unbelievably, the buck stops at twenty-two yards—broadside. I draw ... he stares but stays. I let fly and hear the unmistakable, whack-a-melon sound of an arrow striking the body cavity. The buck races off, but I have a really good feeling about this one.

I let out some pent-up breath and sit down on the platform. My compact binocular reveals the fletching of the arrow sticking up above the low brush. I have no doubt it is full of buck blood. And there is little doubt this animal is the apparition that stepped out of the fog and into my dreams, waking and sleeping, two weeks earlier.

Few moments in a hunter's life can match that delicious interlude just after a shot that you know was spot-on. With no need to rush off anywhere, you can replay the film in your head and savor each frame. You drink in your surroundings and revel in just being there.

If you're a graying hunter looking ahead to an uncertain future, you feel a deeper connection to this moment. You value, in a way that you may never have realized before, the circumstances that combined to bring you to this place—not just this now-magical corner of the woods but this place in your life. You accept with gratitude this blessing you've been graced with here, and perhaps you find it easier to accept the rigors of the aging process. They have tested your mettle, and you have not been found wanting. When tougher tests come, so will other blessings, and other realizations. If you know the source of those blessings, you'll handle it.

I found the sleek animal just yards from my last sight of it. He won't make anybody's record book but mine, but a friend is mounting the head and it will help me to conjure up, whenever I like, the day I came to fully understand how rich and fulfilling my life is.

Perspectives of a "Mature" Hunter

Yes, I guess I am certifiably a codger. The years—especially the last few—have thoroughly whitened the thatch atop my head, dismissed many of the little tuning hairs in my inner ear, and spurred on the irritating creatures that do the sandblasting inside my knees and hips.

But the years and the infirmities have merely mellowed my consuming love of hunting. For me, one of its bedrock values is, for want of a better word, aloneness. How many of us today (or even forty years ago) spend much time truly alone? I don't mean in the bathroom or on a business trip or on a walk in the neighborhood—I mean alone beyond the clutches of humanity's insistent clamor. Beyond the blare of car horns and all the maddening variety of modern communication devices, beyond any human voice save our own, ideally beyond sight of any human habitation. Alone in the natural world.

Hunting (and often fishing) spirits me into that alone world—the real world, as I see it. It is a place of peace, a place where important life lessons, most notably those about self, are somehow magically taken to heart. If an animal should fall to my gun or bow, so much the better, but the knowledge comes, kill or no.

A case in point: One fall morning ten years ago I was perched in full bowhunting camo in a place I called the Squire's Woods in the hills of northern Virginia. Somehow a bobcat appeared just feet from the bottom of my ladder stand. The essence of stealth, it had materialized without making a sound—which even I would have heard, given the dried-up leaves of early autumn. One foot up on a rock, the other raised and motionless, intense yellow eyes lasering into mine, it stared for a moment before moving off as furtive as the wildest predator in Africa.

I took no game meat for the freezer that morning, but I will remember that hunt for the rest of my days.

I don't know who first said it, but one of my all-time favorite expressions is, "Life is an adventure—live it!" Which points up hunting's Number One attraction for me: This sport has taken me to many of the premier adventures of my seven-plus decades on this old orb of travail. Try this one on:

Back during the too-short time when I was managing editor of the NRA's *American Hunter* magazine, the bigs sent me to North Dakota to test a new shotgun on the overabundant hordes of snow geese making their way south from their breeding grounds in Canada. Well before first light I helped set out literally hundreds of decoys on a vast stubblefield, then ensconced myself under a big white plastic "hide" contoured to look like a snow goose on steroids.

As first light colored the eastern sky, wave after wave of dark shapes left the marsh and rose into that red sky. It was almost impossible to conceive of the sheer numbers of birds in those rising ranks. And they were heading right toward the dozen or so shooters waiting below.

The leading flanks spotted the flock of phonies on the ground and began to circle overhead. More and more and more geese joined them until the incredible funnel cloud numbered certainly 5,000 and maybe as many as 10,000 snow and blue geese. The vortex of birds continually lowered, their throaty calls obliterating every other sound.

Somebody may have yelled, "Take 'em!" but I never heard it. I did, though, feel the ground shudder when an eight-pound white missile slammed down less than a yard from my head. I flipped over my blind and began blamming away, trying my best to sort out single birds from the unimaginable melee above. Geese rained down incessantly until the incredible white tornado gradually lifted away and dissipated.

That, folks, was an *adventure*.

There is a flip side to the aloneness factor cited above. Though it is certainly not a spectator sport, hunting has an uncanny ability to generate and nurture lifelong friendships. I am hugely blessed to have a handful of friends who share my affair with hunting and the outdoors. In dirt-floored cabins, riverside campsites, and unpeopled wild country from Maine to Mexico, Virginia to Montana, and Florida to Alberta, we've tested ourselves, toasted and roasted each other, laughed until we cried, and come to know the best and the worst about each other. As we all age, these guys become more important to me than ever before. They are more than friends—they are mirrors of me.

'Course, a couple of those guys are gadget gurus—sort of my alter-ego. They bust me about my beat-up guns, my emphasis on stealth in the woods, and my lack of "hunter aids"—you know, the Wal-Mart approach to woodsmanship. I'm not buying it—literally. But I forgive them, because friends are far higher on my list of hunting's rewards than the size of a rack or a full bird bag.

One of those friends, Vin Sparano, can attest to the following story. Back in what my kids would call the Dark Ages, the late 1960s and seventies, he and I toiled on the editorial staff of *Outdoor Life* magazine in New York. (Vin later was named editor-in-chief.) I was thrilled to get that job—imagine touching pencil to copy written by the likes of Jack O'Connor, OL's long-time hunting editor!

A quick story about O'Connor: He and his wife Eleanor (he called her the War Department) visited our offices one morning, and Jack plopped himself down at the desk of managing editor Chet Fish (yep, that was really his name). Deaf as a post from years of shooting without ear protection (nobody worried about that back then), and totally outspoken, he bellowed, "SAY, CHET, WHAT'S A GUY LIKE YOU MAKE A YEAR ANYWAY?"

I don't remember Chet's reply, but I acutely recall the profound silence that followed from us peons out in the bullpen nearby—not a typewriter clack (this was well before computers), not a footfall, not even a snicker.

O'Connor was a hoot, but interacting with him and other giants of the outdoor field of that era—Charlie Elliott, Ben East, Jim Carmichel, and Jim Zumbo (Jim Z and I later became great friends, still are)—ensured that hunting was seared into my soul.

Hunting has graced my life, from my teenaged years of chasing rabbits and pheasants with a bird-busting beagle named Kelly to a confrontation with a fine muley buck last fall in Montana. Over that span, I've lost my urge to limit out (not that I did so very often) and now measure success in terms of bobcat sightings and belly laughs and bourbon in a glass after a day afield. And a plateful of Venison Artichoke that I prepare myself ain't hardly bad either.

Such things make it a bit easier to accept the rigors of the aging process. I don't know where the path ahead will lead (though I know Who is leading the way). But whatever the future may hold for me, one thing will not change: Hunting will remain embedded in the soul of who I am.

Hunting as a Rite of Passage

Is hunting good for kids? Why do they do it? Is it sport or is it instinctive? Does hunting encourage violence or does it teach empathy and compassion? Would it be a more peaceful world if more men hunted? These are some of the questions addressed in a new book entitled *From Boys to Men of Heart: Hunting as Rite of Passage.*

Award-winning author Randall L. Eaton is a behavioral scientist with an international reputation in wildlife conservation who has been studying hunting for thirty-five years. While producing "The Sacred Hunt" in the mid-1990s, he interviewed scores of recreational hunters as well as Native Americans. Eaton was surprised to discover that they all used the word "respect" to describe how they feel about animals they hunt.

That prompted Eaton to conduct questionnaire surveys on thousands of mature hunters who described their attitude toward animals they hunt as "respect, admiration, and reverence." More than eighty percent of the hunters claimed they prayed for the animals they killed or gave thanks to God.

Eaton's survey also asked hunters what life event most opened their hearts and engendered compassion in them. The choices included death of a loved one, death of a beloved pet, becoming a parent, taking the life of an animal, and teaching young people. The women hunters overwhelmingly chose "becoming a parent," but nearly all the men selected taking the life of an animal.

"These results indicate the fundamental polarity of human life. Women are adapted to bringing life into the world, but men are adapted to taking life in order to support life," Eaton said.

The same survey asked respondents to choose those universal virtues they learned from hunting. The top three choices were inner peace, patience, and humility.

Eaton's book contains interviews of leading authorities in several fields who corroborate his research. One is Michael Gurian, family therapist and best-selling author of several books on how to properly raise boys. Gurian agrees that hunting does teach men compassion, and that it would be a more peaceful world if more men hunted. The Gurian Institute recommends Eaton's book to parents.

"Hunting is counter-intuitive," said Eaton, "because people who haven't had the experience can't imagine that it opens the heart and awakens a moral sense."

As Eaton took calls on a national radio show, a distraught woman told him, "You're just teaching kids violence!" He responded, "What do you think Jimmy Carter and Nelson Mandela would say? They won the Nobel Peace Prize and both are avid hunters."

Also mentioned in his hunter's hall of fame are Teddy Roosevelt, among the world's greatest conservationists, Thomas Jefferson, Audubon, Thoreau, Aldo Leopold, John Steinbeck, Jimmy Stewart, and Shaq O'Neal.

Eaton quotes Dr. Don T. Jacobs, professor of education and author of Teaching Virtues Across the Curriculum, as concluding, "Hunting is the ideal way to teach young people universal virtues including courage, fortitude, patience, generosity, and humility. Humility," Jacobs adds, "is discovering that you're part of something greater than yourself."

The book presents compelling evidence that hunting is an inherited instinct. Eaton believes that for boys at least, hunting definitely is not sport but an instinct. He compares hunting to sex:

"Sex drives a young male toward a sexual encounter, but a surprise awaits him. Sooner or later he falls in love. The instinct links up with the heart. It is a transformative experience with enormous consequences including marriage, parenting, and providing. The instinct to hunt propels a young man to pursue the animal, but a surprise comes when he takes its life and his heart is opened. He discovers first-hand the interdependence of life. That is how males fall in love with nature and why they are the leaders in conservation."

Adolescent males, Eaton argues, need rites of passage to become responsible adults. He believes the original rite of passage was hunting because it proved that a male could provide and qualify for manhood and marriage. He believes it still is the ideal path by which boys may become men of heart. He also recommends wilderness survival and vision quest, always with appropriate mentoring.

Eaton's book claims that hunting also develops character, values, and virtues in girls and profoundly connects them with nature. If it is so good for youth, then why are the ranks of hunters declining?

"One factor," Eaton suggests, "is fear of guns. How many parents and teachers know that hunting is the safest form of outdoor recreation?"

The book refers to the work of Dr. Helen Smith, author of *Scarred Hearts* and the world's leading expert on youth violence, who says that access to firearms does not cause youth violence. She believes that teenagers need boundaries and responsibility, which shooting and hunting provide when mentored by adults. She suspects that the Columbine tragedy never would have happened had the boys been properly mentored in hunting and shooting.

Eaton is glad about the "No Child Left Inside" movement, inspired by Richard Louv's book, *The Last Child in the Woods*.

"It's a good thing for kids to spend more time outside, but I doubt that the connection they make with nature is deep enough to promote a conservation ethic." In his opinion, "Not only are hunting and fishing better for kids, kids who hunt and fish are better for the environment."

According to Eaton, hunting is justifiable in terms of its enormous economic impacts and benefits to environmental conservation. He said, "We all take life, but for those who participate directly in it, the food chain becomes a love chain. Look at Ducks Unlimited. They've permanently conserved over twelve million acres of wetlands throughout North America to the benefit of the entire living community. In just a few years, the Rocky Mountain Elk Foundation has conserved over four million acres for wildlife and successfully reintroduced elk to the eastern U.S."

He sees most of the environmental community engaged in rearguard actions while the hunting and fishing community is on the offensive.

Eaton's 336-page book is available from OWLink Media. For more information, contact Dr. Randall Eaton at 513-244-2826 or at reaton@eoni.com.

Mystique of the Mule Deer

**The big gray deer with the pogo-stick gait and the superb
antlers is an icon of places high, wild, and free.**

I might as well come clean right up here at the top: I'm an eastern
dude with a whole lot of time spent in the whitetail woods. The big
gray deer of the wide and lonesome West has brightened far too few
of my days, and I am certainly no oracle on the nuances of finding
the largest of his kind.

I write this rather in an attempt to describe the mystique of the
mule deer—the facts and fables that help to define this unique animal
and the see-forever country that so often seems to swallow him up.
Maybe an easterner with no preconceptions—and a far different kind
of deer to use as a comparison—is a good person to write about the
special qualities of the muley.

A case in point: A couple of years ago, buddy Rick Crouse and
I—he from Maryland, I from Virginia—made a long-anticipated trip
to northwest Wyoming. The day before the mule deer opener, we
trudged along a trail through a piece of BLM land that looked as if it
couldn't hide a jackrabbit—a little sage, a few pinyon pines, and lots
of crumbling red rock that typify the undulating slopes that shoulder
gradually up from the valley of the Shoshone River and form the base
of magnificent timbered escarpments and, beyond, the 10,000-foot
peaks of the North Absaroka Wilderness Area.

"This ain't Virginia, Crouse," I said, and his answering grunt was
affirming if not eloquent as we stopped to drink in the superb pan-
oramas on all sides. It was all we could do to stop gawking and concentrate on glassing the country nearby for the mule deer bucks old
friend Jim Zumbo—who *is* an oracle when it comes to mule deer—
said we might find here.

It takes a while for a Virginian to become convinced that a deer—
and a *big* deer for that matter, weighing on average one-third more
than a whitetail—would be able to "hide" in such barren terrain. But
as we stood there glassing, Rick picked up movement just under a
ridgeline some 400 yards away. A small group of deer stood there

looking back over their shoulders at us. Even at that distance, we could see that one carried a hatrack on his head. We two groups stared at one another until a snow squall blew up the valley and erased them from sight, though not from memory.

Rick and I were there at first light the next morning, armed, ready, and fired up, but we never saw that buster again. We did, though, find his tracks well before dawn on a subsequent morning, and learned once again that big bucks get big by following nocturnal feeding schedules and lying up where hunters can't or won't go.

That incident points up some of the traits that make the gray deer an icon of the mountain West. He is a deer of the distance. He prefers to live in open country—maybe because he likes the scenery as much as hunters do, but mostly because it allows him to use his wonderful eyes and big antenna-dish ears to key in on approaching danger. It's a humbling experience to hump up to the edge of a high ridge, peer over ever so slowly and carefully, and see a group of muleys riveted on the top three inches of your camouflaged but skylined head and ready to race away. Whitetails have wonderful eyesight, but the muley's is simply uncanny. It allows him to use distance the way a whitetail uses cover and stealth.

A shoulder mount of this magnificent mule deer conjures instant memories of Montana's high and wild.

The mule deer is a gregarious critter. Except during the rut, he likes the company of his own kind and almost always travels in groups. Bachelor bunches of bucks numbering two to seven are common. Oh, there are a few grizzled old loners that keep to themselves way up in the high country or in the worst of the badlands, but these "ridge-runners" are rare. And they almost always haul around a set of antlers that would make your jaw drop.

Yeah, those antlers! It doesn't take an exceptional set of muley antlers to make me and most other easterners salivate. In fact, more than a few experts recommend that a mule deer first-timer *leave his gun unloaded* for the first day or two, until he has seen a few big gray bucks.

It takes a whole lot of personal discipline to avoid whanging away at the first buck you see. Here's how Jim Zumbo puts it: "If you're the type of person who hyperventilates when a big-racked deer shows up, then you'd better have an oxygen bottle handy when you see your first really big muley buck. The antlers are typically very high, wider than most whitetails you've ever looked at, and a sight to behold when the buck wearing them lumbers away in his peculiar gait, which makes the rack seem even bigger."

Zumbo should know. He has spent most of a lifetime chasing muleys, and has written one of the definitive books on the subject: *Hunting America's Mule Deer*. Much of his how-to knowledge is crammed into a video, *Jim Zumbo's Secrets to Success: Mule Deer*.

I'm surprised he himself doesn't *doink-doink-doink* across the sagebrush flats in the muley's weird pogo-stick gait that the biologists call stotting. It may look like a muley buck's got a hitch in his git-along as he bounces away from you, all four of his feet off the ground during each of the stotts, or jumps. But that strange gait not only gobbles up the yardage but also seems to accentuate the animal's antlers, the tines of which fork instead of growing individually up from a main beam as on the whitetail.

The mule deer's historic faith in distance will be attested to by generations of hunters who have watched a good buck bounce away, only to stop out there for a final look back at its pursuer. Often it would pause within decent rifle range, and become part of the hunter's winter meat supply.

But these days the great gray deer is wising up, stretching out his escape run and often disappearing over the nearest ridge without checking back on the guy with the boom-stick. He seems, too, to be orienting more and more to thicker cover, particularly in the hours of full daylight. I fervently hope the muley will not mutate to become essentially a western whitetail, skulking about in the thick stuff, stealthy and introverted.

Nah, that's not gonna happen. The nature of the animal and the places he graces will see to that. The mule deer is a stand-up creature that leaves his tracks in lands where the people who seek him feel free and unfettered and uplifted and challenged—whether those lands are rolling sage flats or contorted badlands or sky-touching high country.

During a recent November, one of the warmest on record in the intermountain West, Rick and I climbed up out of the Shoshone Valley to reach the receding snowline, where we knew the bucks were hanging to escape the unseasonable warmth. Sore-footed and sweating, we topped a high ridge and sat in the shade of a lone pinyon pine. All around us, a full 360 degrees, were jagged, snowy peaks, from the relatively nearby Absarokas to the Grand Tetons seventy miles away. In a snow patch at our feet were the new tracks of a large mule deer, complete with dewclaws.

It was entirely enough.

Perils and Pratfalls of Pro Photographers

The wanderings of those who would capture the essence of wild country and its critters with their lenses are fraught with emotions ranging from throat-clenching fear to laugh-out-loud folly.

Not many months ago as this is written, Idaho-based shutterbug Tim Christie and I spent a few days roaming around in Banff and Jasper national parks in the province of Alberta in western Canada. Winter was beginning to release its relentless grip, the craggy magnificence of that country sparkled against a cobalt-blue sky, and the hardy creatures that live there were out and about, sucking up the sun like human snowbirds from Santa Barbara.

I had jumped at Tim's invitation–for a variety of reasons. As an eastern flatlander, I'm enamored of mountains, and these Alberta high-rises are *mountains*. I haven't spent a whole lot of time cheek by jowl with the likes of bighorn sheep, mountain goats, elk, and wolves, and always wanted to. And some forty years in the outdoor writing/editing business have instilled deep within me the idea that some indefinable mystique surrounds people who make all or part of their living photographing wild creatures where they live. I've always suspicioned that pro photogs have a hidden stash of some rare and valuable knowledge and are keeping it a secret from me. Yeah, I guess I should see a shrink.

My odyssey with Christie–which featured encounters with bighorns and bull elk, ptarmigan and eagles—did not dispel that notion entirely. But from Tim and others in his business I've heard some wild tales of trials and tribulations and downright throat-tightening terror that make me less jealous of their wanderings. And a couple of these guys have had arm-flailing, nose-bleeding, guffaw-producing days that make them seem almost as human as, well, me! Here's a sampling:

FOOTSIE WITH A GRIZ

Tim Christie lives with his wife Kathy and three golden retrievers in Coeur d'Alene, Idaho. He is also a professor of communications and teaches a class in nature photography at Northern Idaho College. His photos, especially of grizzlies, have graced the covers of many magazines over the past three decades. Tim@timchristiephoto.com

It was 10:30 a.m. on October 5, 1986 in the west end of Glacier Park—he'll never forget those details. The light was poor for photography, but as he moseyed along in his pickup he spotted a big whitetail buck hot on a doe, ignoring the observer. Not wanting to take the time to replace his Nikes with boots, Tim grabbed five rolls of film and his camera with a honking big 300mm lens and followed the deer, which allowed him to record their amore for nearly an hour from twenty to forty yards.

Back toward the truck, which was 200 yards off, he heard brush crack. The buck got nervous and bolted away. As Tim put the tripod over his shoulder to head back, he heard a high-pitched bawl and the brown blur of bear cubs running. "Oh, bad word–a griz!" he remembers saying aloud. This was in the pre-bear-spray days.

Without hesitation he climbed the only sizable tree around, a fir ten to twelve inches across and about forty feet tall. Right now here came Mama–teeth popping and snarling and growling like a junkyard dog. She hit the tree hard enough to make it sway violently, and up she came. "Don't let anyone tell you a grizzly can't climb trees," Tim says.

Tim hung on for dear life about eighteen feet up, with the toe of his right foot pointed down and the heel upward. The sow, obviously enraged and hot for revenge, lunged up and grabbed that right sneaker. He felt himself being pulled downward, but then the sneaker came off (darned good thing he hadn't put his boots on). Apparently the downward momentum caused a branch she was standing on to break, and down she went, stripping off all the other branches on the way and thudding to the forest floor.

Still thoroughly incensed, the bear climbed a nearby leaner and glared at the man from twenty yards. She was a large silvertip animal, and Tim couldn't help thinking: *What beautiful eyes*. She dropped to the ground with a loud *Woof!* and disappeared. He was up there for an hour and a half, and getting down the limbless tree just added to his scrapes and bruises. On the other hand, he was alive. He told me that at virtually the same hour, another photographer was killed and eaten by a grizzly in Yellowstone.

THE DAY FROM HELL

Gary Kramer of Willows, California, worked for many years with the U.S. Fish and Wildlife Service before chucking it all to become a full-time photographer and writer. His latest creation, A Ducks Unlimited Guide to Hunting Diving and Sea Ducks, *is available through his website, www.garykramer.net.*

The time: late April, 2002. The place: desert north of Lordsburg, New Mexico. The characters: one professional photographer and two wildlife biologists (names have been changed to protect the inno-cent–and the chagrined). The mission: you decide.

The photographer's primary target was desert bighorn sheep, but they weren't cooperating. So when he ran into a young wildlife biol-ogist–we'll call him Chuck–who was studying the area's elusive Gila monsters, our hero's interest was piqued. The large orange-and-black lizard isn't something you see–or have a chance to get on film–every day, and the biologist was studying the reclusive critters with the aid of radio transmitters implanted in a half-dozen or so.

Gary tagged along and exposed five or six rolls as the biologist used telemetry gear to locate one of the venomous Gila monsters. Gary noted how the biologist grabbed and handled the lizard–a fact the reader should keep in mind as our tale evolves.

The lizard caper made the photographer lose track of time, but he finally realized that he was late for a date with another biologist to locate a prairie-chicken lek (breeding ground) on the other side of the state. So he mounted up his rental Chevy Blazer and headed across the barren desert headed east. A flat tire made him even later.

And then, as he drove down a dry wash, he saw an enormous Gila monster heading in the same direction. Here was another unique photo op, so he stopped the rig, jumped out, and, recalling how the biologist did it, grabbed the big lizard behind the neck. This reptile was at least as long as his forearm, and remember, the Gila is poisonous, subduing its victims by masticating their flesh.

The dry wash was a poor place for photos, so Gary placed the Gila on the seat beside him, kept his hand pressed down on it, and drove off, looking for a place with some structure and vegetation to make a pleasing setup.

Here the plot thickens. Not much farther along, a large rock became dislodged from the steep wall of the wash, just missed a front wheel, and lodged in an immovable position in front of a rear wheel. The car was moving at only fifteen mph, but it stopped so suddenly that Gary's face smashed hard against the stem of the steering wheel. Now he has "a nose bigger than W.C. Fields' that is bleeding profusely and eyes watering so bad I can hardly see."

The critter? Still in place on the seat, Gary's hand holding it there. Stupefied by the jolt and yet incredulous, he recalls saying aloud: "What the hell am I doing with this animal?" Finally he recomposed himself, released the lizard, stuffed a large wad of tissue up each nostril to stanch the blood flow (where it stayed for three hours), and moved out. He raced across the state, knowing he would never be able to keep his appointment. Luckily, he was able to locate the lek area on his own, in the dunes outside Roswell.

Plot thickens further: The plan was to set up a photo blind, leave it, and come back in the morning in hopes of capturing on film the fascinating and unique mating dance of the prairie chickens. But as he stepped out of the now dented rental car, he inadvertently hit the lock button just as the relentless New Mexico wind slammed the door. Car's running, keys are inside, gas tank's almost full, daylight is almost gone. Now tears of laughter blend with the tears of pain.

The only option was to break a window. But there wasn't a rock in sight and he was simply too beat up to break the window with an elbow or foot. After a full hour, in the dark, he found an old fence post and was able to bust a window.

Repair of one broken window: $250. Reworked contract on the rental car: couple hundred. The pain and suffering required to get critter photos–priceless!

DEATH BY COW?

Bill Lea of Franklin, North Carolina is a wildlife/natural resources photographer and Vice President of the American Bear Association. He is perhaps best known for his shots of deer and bear behavior, the Great Smoky Mountains, and southern ecosystems. www.BillLea.com.

About fifteen years ago Bill was wandering in Tennessee's Great Smoky Mountains National Park with his camera when he spied a black bear up in an oak tree stuffing its face with acorns. The large, open-grown white oak was in a sprawling pasture, and a sizable herd of cattle munched grass on a hill a few hundred feet away (back in those days, the park still leased out some land for cattle grazing).

The adolescent bear was deep within the shade of the branches, so Bill casually set up his tripod, mounted the camera, and relaxed in the beauty of the September day. With no warning, the bruin suddenly barreled down the oak and ran off. Lea couldn't figure that out—until the entire herd of bovines took off at a dead run—straight toward him. It took only a moment to realize that those cattle–the herd mentality by now in full swing–were after that bear, which they obviously saw as an enemy.

Bill, out in the open with nothing to hide behind, was between the stampeding herd and the lumbering bruin. He recalls thinking, *Am I gonna die by cow? That's embarrassing!*

He stood perfectly still. The ground shook as the heavy animals caught up to him and—much to his surprise and relief—simply flowed around him. That bear had sensed what was about to happen and got out of Dodge while the getting was good.

YOU KNOW IT'S GONNA BE A BAD DAY WHEN...

Ron Spomer of Bloomington, Indiana, a Field Editor for American Hunter *magazine and frequent contributor to many other outdoor publications, is a guru of western gamebirds and dogs that hunt them, ungulates, hunting optics, digital cameras, and too many other subjects to mess with here. www.ronspomeroutdoors.com/photo/*

Ron described for me a series of quick-advance exposures that reminded me of a whirlwind bird shoot we shared in South Dakota a while back. Never knew another guy who could shoot pictures and ducks at the same time. I'll let him tell it:

"There was the time I set out on a recently thawed Dakota wetland in a float tube to photo redheads and promptly lost a swim fin—which meant I was reduced to spinning in circles. This would only have resulted in a long float out, except that the tube started leaking, leading to a frantic, minimally effective kicking/steering motion with both feet and one arm while trying to keep camera and long lens high and dry with the other. Toes touched bottom about the same time water began lapping over the waders. Alas, I survived."

Another time years earlier, the newly minted shutterbug set up his new camera and newfangled motor drive in a shallow wetland, lens trained on a perch favored by singing redwing blackbirds. Then he walked 150 feet away, unrolling that much copper wire through which his shutter-tripping electronic signal would travel. Unfortunately, one leg of his tripod sank in the muck quicker than the two others, and the big lens hit the soup face-first. Fortunately, the metal lens hood and shallow water prevented serious submersion.

"Which brings to mind," he says, "wading through flooded Arkansas timber, Canon camera body, zoom lens, and flash in hand, maneuvering for shots of hunters swinging on ducks, Labs fetching, etc. My foot found a submerged log just at that critical point where my forward momentum could be stopped only by placing said foot ahead of said log. The log didn't budge, so I went in—but not face-first. No, with the speed and grace of an Olympian gymnast, I turned and went in back-first, right arm shooting upward to extend the camera above the water. This might have worked if the darned neck strap hadn't stopped upward progress. Minnows were swimming in the lens."

Finally—perhaps mercifully so—he adds: "Despite crawling flat on my belly within striking distance of rattlesnakes, and getting between two fighting bull moose, I've had no near-death experiences—unless you count the time in Canada when a bull elk overdosed on testosterone took offense at my big lens pointing at his favorite cow and rushed me. My only injury was a torqued back from leaping, turning, and fleeing faster than my stiff old muscles were able to handle."

CASE OF THE PSYCHOTIC MULEY

Tim Flanigan of Bedford, Pennsylvania, doubles as a wildlife conservation officer and a professional photographer. One of his specialty areas is animal diseases, abnormalities, and mishaps. The story below transcends "mishap." NatureExposure@comcast.net

The winter's first substantial snowfall created prime conditions for a photo shoot in a large enclosure at a southern Pennsy deer-prop-agation facility. Tim mounted his big 300mm lens atop a heavy tripod and focused on a large mule deer buck pacing and posturing about twenty feet away. The lens revealed not only large, high antler tines but also bulging eyes, an erect neck mane, and big ears flat against a swollen neck—the buck was obviously still in rut, though it was early January. Tim's been around the block with wild creatures—and a few wild humans—over the past three decades and wasn't concerned. Big mistake.

Triggered by what Tim believes was the buck's seeing his reflection in the big, threatening "eye" of the camera lens, the animal suddenly charged, driving his long antlers into the tripod legs, tossing the whole shebang over the now-on-his-butt man's shoulder, and ramming his nose and antlers down into Tim's groin. The man was stunned and breathless for a few seconds but then looked down to see that a ten-inch tine appeared to have penetrated his left groin and punched through three layers of clothing to emerge on the other side. A matching tine was doing a job on the right groin area. The buck was wildly thrashing his large rack back and forth and pushing downward with incredible power, twin jets of vapor spewing from his nostrils.

Within reach was a two-foot section of pine two by four, and Tim used it to club the animal repeatedly between the antlers, trying to minimize the thrashing by grabbing one of them with his free hand. The buck seemed oblivious, and in a few minutes Tim was exhausted and could no longer hold the club. When he stopped struggling, so did the buck, which tried to back away but couldn't free his antlers from the layers of heavy clothing–which sent him into a panicked rage that battered the man's arms and ribs.

Long minutes later the combatants separated, and Tim was able to stagger to minimal protection in the angle where an oil tank leaned against a shed. His movement, however, just seemed to rekindle the animal's murderous rage. It chased him from that refuge to a pile of firewood (the buck demolished it), a stack of heavy chain-link-fence rolls (the whacked-out deer repeatedly lifted and dropped the ends of those rolls with his forehead and antlers), and a big maple tree set amid heavy growth of multiflora rose (which ended up shredded). At each "safe house," Tim noticed that direct eye contact seemed to re-energize the 250-pound animal.

Long story short, the man finally escaped into another pen and found that, though battered, bruised, and scraped, he had not been gored. What's the use of being Irish if you can't be "lucky" once in a while?

"LEAVE US ALONE!"

Bill McRae of Choteau, Montana, has been photographing wild creatures, especially ungulates and large carnivores, for close to half a century. He'll tell you without hesitation that most wild animals are potentially dangerous. bmcrae@3rivers.net.

Denali National Park in Alaska can be incomparably beautiful in early September—the tundra putting on a shameless display of yellow, purple, red, and orange, sunrays uninhibited by air pollution encrusting starbursts on every leaf, twig, and blade of grass. It was like that more than twenty years ago when Bill and another wildlife photographer, Elroy Nelson, began setting up to film an exceptional bull moose with a cow near Igloo Creek within a quarter-mile of the Denali Highway.

As they readied their equipment, the cow, which had been lying in a spruce thicket, jumped up and started moving away. When Bill made an innocuous arm movement, the bull—which probably weighed 1,500 pounds—moved up beside the cow and seemed to be glaring at the man. Seconds later, without warning, the hulking black animal charged full-throttle at Bill. Here's how he tells it:

"At times such as this, one's legs have a mind of their own, and mine had me turned and running before I knew what had happened. I dashed for about 100 feet and started to swerve behind a spruce tree when I tripped! As I went sprawling, with expensive Nikon cameras crashing together, I glanced over my shoulder, afraid I was about to be trampled by the bull. He wasn't there!

"He had pursued me for about thirty feet, then swung in a circle and charged Elroy, following him only a short distance. I stood up on legs that felt like jelly, thankful to be unharmed. The bull glared at us for a few minutes and then went back to the cow. All he had really said was, 'Go away and leave us alone.' We did!"

And he adds: "No wildlife photograph is worth dying for." To date, he has known four photographers who have been killed while filming grizzly bears.

Chapter 6

DEFINING SUCCESS

Fishing's rewards are legion, and not the least of them is the chance to dine on fillets of walleye or salmon or smallmouth bass caught from waters you can see as you eat—complemented, of course, with a good wine.

Jesus, too, was partial to fish—and wine. When a crowd of some 5,000 people walked a long way from the nearest town to hear Him speak, He fed them all with about a dozen fish and a few loaves of bread. And a little later, when the wine was running out at a wedding reception in the town of Cana, also in Galilee, He was the hit of the party when He transformed many gallons of water into fine wine—and got chewed out for saving the best for last.

He saved the best of His life for last, too. Every week I eat a meal that is much more fulfilling than the best fillet. It's a little wafer of bread and maybe a sip of wine, transformed into Christ's body and blood. They symbolize and celebrate the end of His life—the greatest act of love in the history of humanity. But before He spread out His arms to encompass us all and be nailed to the wooden crosspieces, He made sure that He had enlisted a bunch of uneducated fishermen to bring His Truth to us. He made them fishers of men.

What's that mean? Pro fisherman and luremaker Cotton Cordell puts it this way: First, teach young people to love God. Then teach them to love their family. Finally, teach them to fish.

And by the time they reach their teens, no dope peddler under the sun will ever have a chance to teach them anything.

The Porch at Old Rag

> **The changeless old house nurtures in its visitors an appreciation of nature's moods and majesty and an understanding of what is truly important in life.**

Since the floor was fixed, we don't see the little snake heads anymore. They used to rise up like miniature periscopes through holes in the rotting edges of the ancient boards, apparently curious about the clumping sounds above their dank and shaded haven under the old porch. Garter and black snakes mostly, they were conversation pieces and part of the ambience of the place.

Other icons help define this haven for humans as well as serpents: the foot-long cutouts of trout and fishing flies jigsawed out of one by tens that form a sort of railing around the porch; the battered flyswatters responsible for the demise of untold generations of buzzing critters that like the porch as much as we do and find the decrepit screens no obstacle to entry; the antique under-eave thermometer that told you how hot or cold it was, within fifteen degrees or so.

Work weekend at the Old Rag Club.

But the central feature of the porch—the first-class seating on our earthbound airship—is the grouping of wooden rocking chairs donated to the Old Rag Mountain Sportsman's Club by one of the members. In all but the bitterest weather, those chairs are the unofficial gathering place for the fifteen or so families or individuals who pay their pittance dues and thereby gain the right to reserve time at the "The Club"—a spartan farmhouse built at the turn of the century and later used to house a few of the people moved out of the Blue Ridge mountains when Virginia's Shenandoah National Park was established in the late 1920s and early thirties.

Recently insulated and vinyl-sided, the weathered but solid old building nonetheless regales its visitors with reminders of an earlier age. Heat is generated by a wonderful stone fireplace—its mantel artfully inscribed "The friends of our friends are our friends"—and by a cast-iron woodburning stove in the kitchen. To cool off on the dog days, you strip down as far as you dare, and bring fans. Or you can walk a couple hundred yards and splash around in one of two laughing little streams that tumble clear and cool out of Shenandoah Park.

Gotta go? Sorry, unless you're up to parking your butt on what used to be called a thunder mug in one of the four upstairs bedrooms, you'll have to head out back to "the facility"—another icon of The Club. A one-holer complete with coffee cans to keep the mice out of the TP, it's a place with its own little window on the mountains—and an uncanny ability to open a window to the inner self. Best of all, you don't even have to flush.

Oh, there's running water inside the clubhouse—all of it cold and flowing from a single spigot into an ancient sink. But it's the best water you'll ever taste, running gravity-driven through a two-inch line embedded in an old wine barrel set deep in a welling spring a quarter-mile up the mountain.

So, you might ask—what are the attractions here? An outhouse and a rocking chair and some spring water just don't do it for you, huh? Well, you can wake up refreshed on a bright spring or fall morning, brew up some hairy-chested coffee, lace up your hiking shoes, and walk up through the backyard to the trail up Old Rag Mountain, one of the best climbs in the area. Or grab a flyrod or an ultralight spinning rod and try for trout—native and stocked—in any number of trout streams, both in and below the Park. When autumn turns the forest russet and gold, ruffed grouse prowl the copses and whitetail bucks rub new-grown antlers on saplings all up and down the hollows.

Fish Dog: Sam on the Porch.

But the attractions of this special place are best assessed from the clubhouse porch. Here the rocker jockey inexorably sheds the chaos and the clutter of city life and comes instead to sense the moods of the mountains: roaring winds, downpours pounding on the tin roof, fog wisping along the mountain faces, the grace-filled days of spring and fall. The seasons aren't truly experienced in the cities and towns— but here they play and prance and display their wares, written in the sky and in the forest and in the blue skeins of water that pulse like veins down the contours of this lovely land. The trees send out their little green offspring, and they grow lush and hide the mountains and the sky for a time. And then the world turns and the days shorten and the trees shed their clothes and the view lengthens and the antlers grow and the human heart is restless, uncertain, reminded of the dying time but somehow enervated by some dimly felt sense of harvest and haven.

We almost never come here when winter winds howl and snow whitens the land and life seems to ebb and gel. We're spoiled by civility and oil heat and don't want to stoke the fireplace and the kitchen's wood-burning cookstove. But the porch at Old Rag beckons nonetheless, and on mild February weekends we "take a drive" and check out the changeless old house and marvel anew at how people actually lived this way and how tough they must have been and how different life was then, and we sit on the porch in our heavy sweaters and coats and we feel thankful for our warm and convenient homes, and for good friends who understand why we need to come here in all the seasons and all the moods of the mountains.

The perspective from the porch is a sensory delight. Each year we comment on the growth of the dawn redwood planted in the front yard in tribute to Thelma Reed, known to all as Pete. We lost Pete a few years back at the age of ninety-six. The feisty little lady was the widow of one of the earliest club members, a national fly-casting champion. The dawn redwood isn't supposed to grow well in Virginia. And we humans aren't supposed to survive into our tenth decade. So much for generalities.

On a moonless late-spring night, my sidekick Sam, a Labrador and the finest nonhuman creature in all the civilized world, prowls the property, visible only as movement blacker than the rest of the night. Finding the perimeter safe and secure, and marking it just to make sure, he returns to the porch to lie at our feet and snore and fart. Outside, hundreds of fireflies light their lamps against the outline of the trees, seeming to compete with the constellations burning in the clear mountain air.

Summer is prime time for a rods-and-cones walk. Here's how to do it: After nightfall, take any group of urban-suburbanites (families with children are prime candidates), find a road/trail/path where there are no manmade lights, and, well, just walk. Oh, yes—no flashlights (except one for the leader, who must not use it until the outcries become truly unbearable). When's the last time *you* exposed yourself to darkness for more than thirty seconds? Given a bit of time, eyes adjust and the night seems less threatening. Don't let the screaming bother you.

The porch is a place to rediscover smells—honeysuckle and woodsmoke, the wonderful moldering odor of the forest floor, morning coffee, hiking sweat. And to hear *real* sounds—birdsong and katydids, pines whispering conspiratorily to a light wind, the baying of a hound hot on a track, the *kuk-kuk-kuk* of a wild turkey, soft human voices with no need to compete with a television.

The metronomic thump of the rocker's curved feet on the floorboards of the old porch seems somehow to evoke echoes...

...the look on the face of Number Two son Brian, ten or twelve then, as we sat out a storm in the big room near the fireplace. With no TV to dull the senses, he stared at the eyes of a decrepit old deer head on the wall, moved to another chair, moved again, and finally said, "I'm going to bed—he keeps watching me!"...

...the bear on the trail that scared the bejaysus out of us...

...the big opening-day trout that everybody marveled at until the "lucky" angler owned up that it was caught in a pay-to-fish pond.

Old stories no less enjoyable in the tenth retelling.

The rhythm of the rocker inevitably makes a man ruminate about the big stuff in his life—the things that drive him, the things he fears, the mistakes he regrets, the people he cherishes. And herein lies the intrinsic value of the porch at Old Rag. In this century-old place in these million-year-old mountains, there is permanence and peace. And there is a sense—an awareness you can almost touch—of what human life means, of its essential elements, and of Who it is that oversees the life force that makes each of us who we are.

We are in church here on the porch at Old Rag. No priest or minister or rabbi delivers a homily to us here, but we are spoken to nonetheless. The voice is often a whisper, something inside that affirms us or calms us or warns us or perhaps gently prods us in a direction we may or may not want to go. The voice is as real and as honest as any we will ever hear. It is Truth, and we ignore it at our peril.

May the porch be with you.

Cheeky young bear lies down to eat Sam's food.

Bear on the Porch!

Allow me, Dear Reader, to regale you with a report of occurrences at the Old Rag Mountain Sportsmen's Club during the weekend before the Fourth of July a few years back. For the two card-carrying codgers who experienced it, it was a banner weekend in just about all respects, and an affirmation of the saying, "Life is an adventure—live it!"

The old turn-of-the-century farmhouse, which sits on sixty acres that abut Shenandoah National Park, is a wonderful place to escape from the modern world with friends and family.

Lifelong buddy Jack Burke and I, with Sam, my yellow Lab, got there Friday evening, slept the sleep of righteous Irishmen, and greeted the beautiful clear morning with cups of Burke's Black and Scurvy Stuff (he calls it coffee), sipped in rocking chairs on the front porch. Life doesn't get much better'n that—or so we thought.

After breakfast we hiked three-quarters of a mile up into the Park to a deep plunge pool on one of the crystalline streams that froth down out of the mountains. By the time we reached the "Swimming Hole," deepest spot in that entire stream, it was getting warm, so Jack and I stripped down to our shorts and took a dip—and I'm here to tell you that water was COLD! You couldn't prove it by Sam, though, who fetched a thrown stick about 3,000 times and seemed to wear a permanent smile.

That evening we dined on Venison Artichoke—now, I'm not much of a cook, but that recipe is delicious—and put the leavings outside on a plate for Sam. As I let him out of the kitchen to have at it, a black bear lumbered out of the woods about sixty yards away. Sam immediately spotted the animal and charged after him, and the bear turned tail and ran back the way he'd come. Now, this bear wasn't huge; it appeared to weigh about 175 to 200 pounds and I'd call him an adolescent.

I kept yelling "NO!" and thankfully Sam came back. I put him in the house right away, because I figure this critter is coming back—which he does, no more than five minutes later. By this time it's nearly dark. The bear scarfs up the venison on the plate, then heads for the porch. Jack and I are standing at the back door, watching. He comes right up on the porch and starts eating Sam's regular kibble out of his dish, not six feet from us! Then, apparently just to let us know he doesn't think much of these two guys standing there ogling him, he lies down to eat! Cheeky critter!

All this while I'm standing at the back door, open wide enough for me to capture the critter in my digital camera and yet also dart back inside and close the main door if necessary. This animal didn't seem at all aggressive, but he sure wasn't much afraid of us either.

After he knocks off that snack, he wanders around on the porch and finds the plastic container with tomorrow's kibble in it and starts banging it around. Well, I go out and holler at him to beat it, and he sort of does. At least he leaves the porch proper, by way of a board seat between two stacks of firewood. But then he goes around behind the edge of the concrete slab of the porch floor and proceeds to pull out the piles of stovewood so he can again get at the dogfood container. We're laughing at his antics, which are playing out in bear-like slow motion, and I'm taking pix like mad, but then he grabs the container again so I chase him off again.

Well, we must have shadow-danced with that mischievous black hulk for a half-hour before he finally decided there wasn't anything left to eat and wandered off. We didn't see him again, but he dropped two big, mushy, seed-filled calling cards on the path leading out to our shooting range.

The Bigger Picture

Both friend Jack and I are knowledgeable lifelong outdoorsmen who love to watch and interact with wild creatures. So we may have played a bit fast and loose with this bruin, in the eyes of wildlife biologists. Here's some background:

Well more than a million black bears (the only kind found in Virginia) exist in North America, many thousands of them in this state. They now roam ninety of our ninety-nine counties, though people rarely see them because they are secretive and shy—most of the time. An exception is the summer breeding season, when the animals are on the move.

Are black bears dangerous? "Heck, yes, they're dangerous," says Dr. Mike Vaughan, former wildlife sciences professor at Virginia Tech. "They're big, powerful animals and can inflict injury on humans. Fact is, though, they rarely do. They're shy and tend to stay away from people."

If you round a corner in a trail, say, and suddenly come upon a black bear, the best course of action is simply to back away slowly and quietly. Don't run. Once it figures out what you are, it will very likely move off.

As with our encounter at the Old Rag Club, food is almost always the trigger of a run-in with blackie. Their keen sense of smell will draw them to such magnets as suet feeders for birds, apple and cherry trees, campfire cookouts, open dumpsters, and such delicacies as venison artichoke. Remove or neutralize the food source, and your bear troubles will likely disappear into the dusk.

A Few of My Favorite Things

The winter still with us has elicited from the local folks a wide-ranging variety of reactions, judgments, and epithets. For the majority, I'm guessing, it has been the *Winter of Our Discontent*. For others, it has been something out of *The Sound of Music*. I admit to being in the latter group. Here's my personal take on "Snowmageddon":

Snowflakes that stay on my nose and eyelashes . . .

It all began a day short of a week before Christmas. The weather gurus even predicted a "significant snowfall," and their maps depicted that our little mid-Virginia mountain town would be smack in the center of the deepest accumulations. The thought went through what's left of my mind: *We might even have a white Christmas!*

That wish was confirmed at about 8 on the morning of December 20, when Sam, our housemate and the finest nonhuman creature in all the civilized world, and I ventured out for our morning constitutional.

Now, snow is one of my very favorite things—even more so than cream-colored ponies and crisp apple strudels, or brown paper packages tied up with strings. Somehow it seems to cover the evils and imperfections of our world in a pristine white blanket, at least for a time.

But this was far more than a blanket. I measured the depth at twenty-three and a half inches—up to my knees and Sam's yellow neck. And it continued to fall heavily. Talk about snowflakes that stay on my nose and eyelashes—the stuff was falling so thickly it threatened to plaster shut the four openings on my face. Every inch of my bundled-up old carcass—and of course its evils and imperfections—wore white, making it even harder to see where I was going.

Our usual two-mile wander was restricted to about 300 yards, but we plodded up the back steps pleasantly fatigued and somehow uplifted. The ensuing cup of coffee was superb.

In the days that followed, I discovered that our sixteen-year-old, fire-engine-red Jeep Grand Cherokee had suddenly become one of my keenly favored things—in addition, of course, to bright copper kettles and warm woolen mittens. Though it is full of yellow Labrador hair and the detritus of wood-gathering, and its gas mileage is about the equivalent of that of two Priuses, it has many positives going for it:

In fishing weather it is easy to find in the high weeds. And even in two-feet-plus of snow, it is the equivalent of a plow. I kid you not! Thanks to good tires, a trusty four-wheel-drive transmission, and perhaps even the crafty wiles of the codger who drives it—and remembers traveling in snow back fifty-years-plus ago when men were men and the weenies didn't close school because of thirteen flakes—I drove into town the morning after Snowmageddon. Why? Beats me—nothing was open.

To do so, however, I had to dig a runway in front of Big Red. It took about an hour of shoveling a driveway's width of damp, heavy snow twenty-five feet long. But when I cranked her up and got some momentum, I was on my way, pushing snow ahead of the rig just like a Highway Department plow blade that the driver forgot to lower.

Wild geese that fly with the moon on their wings . . .

At 5:30 this very morning, as I write this deathless prose, I awoke from a sound sleep and for some reason couldn't return to the arms of Morpheus (you remember him—he's the guy who started this "morphing" business). A glance outside convinced me it was walk time.

Sam and I meandered up the neighborhood road amid a magical dawn: a brilliant two-thirds moon hung vertically in a southerly aspect, the Big Dipper was still visible overhead, and the first light of a new day was silhouetting the Blue Ridge to the east.

Out of the silence came a single *honk!* Then two more—close together. It was a brace of Canadas, and their sound indicated they were on a collision course with that gibbous moon. Immediately I thought of those words in bold-face above, and conjured up that vision of big birds against the bright moon. It didn't quite happen, but no matter—that early walk made my day.

Silver white winters that melt into springs . . .

The big Christmas snow lasted a long time, but a day or three after it finally disappeared, the forecasters were at it again (I'm convinced they simply get their jollies from occasional meteorological mayhem). No more two-footers, but a series of weather-map red/yellow blobs came marching across the southern states and made a beeline (as in "when the bee stings") for the mid-Atlantic and the Northeast. Eight-incher. Four-incher. Six-incher. A ten-incher. Global Cooling, without a doubt.

Our world remained pristine—well, in theory—until early March, a simply unheard-of phenomenon for most locations on the central eastern seaboard. Somehow we have switched neighborhoods with Idaho—a good friend out there tells me it's been mostly snowless.

One run-in with the white stuff does stick in my craw. Call it "when the dog bites": Rita (AKA Dear Spouse) was getting weary of seeing dog hair and sawdust on her winter coats, so I decided to free up the Camry, a front-wheel (not four-wheel)-drive car we'd squirreled away in the garage. A few square inches of gravel had appeared on the driveway, thanks to some anemic sunshine, and my early successes with Big Red had afflicted me with unwarranted bravado.

Shoveling a runway for takeoff was a lot harder this time, given that the driveway was now mostly ice at least three inches thick and granite-hard. But I gave it a run—and spun to an irrevocable halt ten feet short of the by now well-plowed road, the right side of the car tilting menacingly toward a large sinkhole that gives our lot "character." The guy who plowed the road came to our rescue the next morning.

The snow isn't gone yet, but it's hurting. Only patches remain here in the foothills, but out to the west the mountains still gleam dazzlingly white in the morning sun. I probably shouldn't say this, but I suspect our memorable winter has run its course. I've loved every minute of it, thanks partly to my favorite movie, the music of Richard Rodgers, and the unforgettable lyrics of Oscar Hammerstein.

My Favorite Things

Raindrops on roses and whiskers on kittens
Bright copper kettles and warm woolen mittens
Brown paper packages tied up with strings
These are a few of my favorite things

Cream colored ponies and crisp apple streudels
Doorbells and sleigh bells and schnitzel with noodles
Wild geese that fly with the moon on their wings
These are a few of my favorite things

Girls in white dresses with blue satin sashes
Snowflakes that stay on my nose and eyelashes
Silver-white winters that melt into springs
These are a few of my favorite things

When the dog bites,
When the bee stings,
When I'm feeling sad

I simply remember my favorite things
And then I don't feel so bad

The Grandest Gamefish

**His Highness, the classy Atlantic salmon, is the
flyfisherman's Holy Grail, but not
all is well in the pristine waters he calls home.**

Okay, so there's this silvery, courageous, strikingly handsome
fish, see, and it so bewitches its devotees that they pay a regal ransom
to stand in a stretch of frigid water and cast a fly on the off-chance
that His Eminence may deign to strike.

Is there anything wrong with this picture? Nope. *Salmo salar*
(salar means "leaper"), the Atlantic salmon, is supremely deserving
of the accolades of anglers, as well as the charges leveled by some
that this fish is the piscatorial equivalent of the Rocky Mountain
bighorn sheep—a prize largely limited to the most well-heeled of
sportspeople.

A list of the salmon's chroniclers reads like a who's-who of the
giants of angling lit. No less an authority than Izaak Walton himself
called *salar* "king amongst gamefish." Lee Wulff, Ernie Schwiebert,
Thomas McGuane, and Jack Hemingway, son of Ernest, have each
captured in eloquent words the fish's legendary qualities: denizen of
North America's most pristine waters, demanding of the angler's best
presentations, and capable of big-time brawling—including multiple
jaw-dropping leaps far above the water's surface.

Taking on the Atlantic salmon is largely the realm of the flyfisherman, and his or her challenges are legion. First, there's the dilemma
of trying to entice a creature that is on its spawning run and essentially doesn't care to eat—and doing so with a hook hidden in a bunch
of feathers and fluff. You try to accomplish this with a rod nine to
twelve feet long, attempting to drive your dry (floating) fly or wet
(fished underwater) fly fifty to seventy feet out to precisely the right
spot, often in a substantial wind.

Oh, yes—did I mention that this silvery torpedo is called the "fish
of a thousand casts"? Not only must your presentation be perfect, but
you must possess the patience of Job and the grit of Genghis Khan.
This isn't a sport for the casual caster. Or for the faint of heart—these
magnificent adversaries weigh eight to twelve pounds on average,

twenty-pounders are not uncommon, and hulks of up to eighty-four pounds have been taken. Now, that's a fish that can really tug on your rope!

The rewards of catching a mature Atlantic salmon include the closeup view (and ensuing photos) you gain of the fish's vivid beauty (silvery olive with red spots), superb eating (though the emphasis today is on releasing the fish), and the clearly felt honor of having taken the flyfisher's Holy Grail.

However, like most of the grandest attractions in our world today, not all is well in the land of the Atlantic salmon. Most of the problems stem from the fact that it lives a pretty rugged life. After hatching in freshwater, the fish progress through several growth stages— alevin, parr, fry, and smolt—before moving downstream and into the Atlantic. They migrate to waters off southwest Greenland, where they stay for one or two years, doing their best to elude predators like birds, larger fish, and seals, before making a marathon journey of some 2,500 miles back to their native river to spawn. During the upstream run they leap obstructions as high as twelve feet. Salmon that spend only one winter at sea are called grilse.

The fish's sensitivity to environmental change and its dependence on both freshwater and saltwater habitats have decimated its populations. Environmental pressures, high-seas overfishing, and other factors have totally eliminated or severely reduced the runs over its historic range—freshwater tributaries of the North Atlantic from Ungava Bay southward to Connecticut, and the European coast from Russia's White Sea to Portugal. In just thirty years wild salmon on our Atlantic coast have decreased by more than two-thirds, and the populations in Maine's Downeast rivers and in the Inner Bay of Fundy are now listed as endangered.

Recent years have seen a disturbing surge in "mortality at sea"— salmon failing to turn up in their home rivers after migration. Every fish that fails to return from Greenland represents lost potential for producing thousands of eggs in rivers already crucially underpopulated. And the numbers continue to fall despite voluntary conservation measures and a ban on commercial harvesting in both North America and on ocean feeding grounds. All Atlantic salmon food products are now grown in sea cages by the aquaculture industry.

The North Atlantic Salmon Conservation Organization lists other problems in the mix: acid rain, especially in Nova Scotia; dams that impede spawning runs; commercial harvesting of capelin and sand lance, two of the salmon's primary foods; poaching; insecticides and other chemicals; and even salmon aquaculture itself. Escapees from the aqua-pens compete for food or breed with wild salmon, producing offspring less capable of surviving in the wild.

And then there's "rock snot," a relatively new problem. An invasive single-celled algae also called "Didymo" (short for *Didymosphenia geminata*), native to freshwater lakes and rivers, is capable of rapid surges in population. The tiny critters release a mucilaginous stalk that they use to attach themselves to bottom structure. These stalks can intertwine to form thick, slippery mats that are not at all user-friendly to anglers—hence the moniker rock snot. And the stuff can in some circumstances destroy spawning habitat and stifle production of insect larvae on which juvenile salmon depend.

To make matters worse, it appears that wading fishermen are the primary culprit in the spread of rock snot. Didymo cells can live for months in the felt soles of wading boots and thereby be transmitted to new watersheds. The first major infestation was reported in 2006 in Quebec's Matapedia River, and it has since been detected in seven other salmon rivers in that province.

With all this mayhem going on in their midst, what's a salmon to do? Perhaps a better question is: what's a fisheries biologist to do? In both Canada and the United States a variety of efforts to restore salmon to their native habitats is underway. For example, Atlantic salmon have been introduced successfully in the Great Lakes (they were native to Lake Ontario but turned belly-up there by the late nineteenth century because of overfishing and habitat loss). The fish are stocked annually in most of the big lakes, but the percentage of salmon reproducing naturally is low. In New England they're knocking down obsolete dams and updating others with the latest concepts in fish ladders and other contraptions that have proven effective with West Coast salmon.

Another factor on the plus side is that the Atlantic salmon, unlike the various species of Pacific salmon, is iteropartic—that is, it does not inevitably die after spawning. Though it is the exception rather than the norm, a certain percentage of each year's spawners manage to recondition themselves and are able to return to sea. Some of them repeat the migration and spawning pattern several times.

And finally, there's the landlocked salmon, a subspecies that lives in northern lakes without ever descending to sea. Called *ouananiche* in much of their range, landlocks are smaller than migrating salmon, bulking up to about thirty-five pounds. It was a landlock that treated me to one of the half-dozen or so fishing experiences that I can still conjure up immediately in minute detail in what's left of my mind.

Northern Quebec's Kaniapiskau River was frothing within three inches of the top of my chest waders as I strained to drive out a three-inch streamer fly to a promising lie behind a massive boulder. I don't think it was my thousandth cast, but I was getting angler's elbow when I finally got it all right. The fly found its way to the more or less protected water in the lee of the rock, and suddenly the fish was on.

With little preamble, a silvery, gyrating, nearly three-foot-long missile rocketed—so help me—six feet skyward. For the first time in my life I was looking *upward* at a fish on my line. I no longer remember how long that epic battle lasted, but I finally lip-landed him, and he graced the wall of our living-room until last year, when the last of his ventral fins fell off.

The Atlantic salmon is a fish you can look up to.

Those Tell-All Scales

Many of the vital stats of an Atlantic salmon can be read in its scales. When a young fish emerges from its egg, it wears no scales. But as the fry grows and rudimentary scales develop, concentric rings form on each, much like the growth rings on a tree, and these rings really spill the beans to a fisheries biologist.

In the warm months, when fish feed actively and grow rapidly, the rings are widely spaced. In the cold months, when food is scarce, the space between rings narrows. The secrets the rings reveal include how many years a salmon has spent at sea and how often it has spawned. Scientists also use scales to tell a wild Atlantic salmon from a captive, raised one—a wild fish's irregular growth rings are very different from the regular rings of a hatchery fish. Scales also serve as source material for DNA, opening a window into the genetic relationships between individual salmon. Fortunately, removing scales does no lasting damage to the "interviewee," which can then be released.

Trophy Fish: From Water to Wall

**A few vital steps, starting as soon as you catch
that dream fish of a lifetime,
will insure that it swims along your wall for a long time.**

Even from ninety feet away I could see the crimson belly and white-edged pectoral fins of a brook trout four times bigger than any I'd ever hooked before. He'd struck my spoon at the edge of a heavy current in northern Quebec's Kaniapiscau River and headed ponderously downstream before rolling on top and giving me all the look I needed.

This is the one! I thought. This was the fish I had come 2,000 miles for, the fish conjured up in dreams too numerous to count, the fish coveted right from the day my Dad had got me hooked on this sport so many years before.

I *wanted* this fish—not to eat, not to brag about, but to fill a special place on the wall of our family room and a special place in my compendium of angling memories. This was a fish to look at and remember, again and again, and perhaps to stir the juices of any budding fisherpersons who might see it up there and wonder.

The superb squaretail was well hooked, and I managed to work him to shore and lip-land him. Our Montagnais guide, Charlie, was waiting to dispatch the fish, and as I handed it over I said, "No cut— no cut!" This was a wall-hanger, and I didn't want the fish gutted or cut in any other way. It would be kept on ice and delivered whole to the taxidermist as soon as I got home.

At least, that was the plan. A half-hour later, when it was time to board the big freighter canoe and head back to our tent camp, Charlie hauled from the river a stringer holding my trophy and a couple of other trout, held it aloft, and said, "No cut—no cut!" My dream fish was now gutless and had a large gash on its peerless head where Charlie had put it out of its misery.

I had never filleted a guide before, and though the idea did flash through my mind, I decided that our language differences should not be the cause of an international incident. And luckily, before that memorable fly-in trip was over, I hooked and landed a skybusting

On-the-Wall Wisdom

Virginia taxidermist Lannie Ballard has seen more than his share of fish and game trophies ruined by improper or nonexistent care, and he has some strong opinions about what you should do once that fish trophy comes into the house. He used to put detailed instructions on the back of the contract for each job, but found that they just weren't read. So now he looks each client in the eye and explains the do's and don'ts of trophy care.

Don't put the fish over a fireplace or woodburning stove, or near a radiator or heat-release duct. The heat and dryness will almost certainly cause the skin or fiberglass to expand and contract (skin is worse than fiberglass in this regard); the paint doesn't have the flexibility to expand or contract, so it eventually cracks.

Quit smoking. Well, he's only half serious about that one, but he advises that smoke from cigarettes or cigars or from a woodburner will gradually take that lifelike sheen from a well-done trophy. Frequent cleaning will help.

How do you clean a trophy mount? Gently, carefully, with a dry, soft rag. If necessary, dampen it, or perhaps put on a very light coating of something like lemon oil. Don't use any stronger solution, or you risk damaging the skin or paint. As you clean, be especially careful of the fins and tail—they are easily damaged. If the gills are flared, use an air hose or vacuum to remove the dust there.

A few minutes of care once a month or so will keep your mount—and your memories—fresh and lifelike.

six-pound landlocked salmon that Charlie never got his mitts on and which today graces a wall in my home.

The language barrier is only one of a lineup of factors that can either ruin a potential trophy fish altogether or make it difficult for even the best taxidermist to preserve or recreate it for your wall. Most of the problems result from failure to prevent the fish from spoiling, or damage to the carcass between the catching and the taxidermist's table.

The following advice can ensure that the lunker you've just landed will end up as a wall mount you can be proud of. Most of it applies whether you're fishing in the back of beyond or the local lake.

A good first step is to include a few simple items as part of the gear you take on every fishing trip: a device to weigh and measure your catch on the spot; a small notebook and pen; a quality stringer that will allow you to keep the fish alive as long as possible (assuming you're not fishing in a boat with a live-well); a small knife with a fine, narrow blade (the keychain kind is just right); a couple of sizable plastic bags (the kitchen-trash size is about right unless you're after very large fish like muskellunge or saltwater species); and a terrycloth or similar towel big enough to wrap around that lunker you may catch.

You may not want to carry a camera on every trip, but do take one along anytime a lunker is a good possibility. One of the newer digitals or a compact SLR is ideal.

Okay—the hulking wall fish lies at your feet, and your pulse is beginning to subside. Take out the camera and shoot at least six broadside shots of the fish from directly above—vary the angle a bit so every detail of that side will be clear to the taxidermist. It's important to do this while the fish is still alive and its coloration is vivid and lifelike. If you wait until the fish has been on ice for a while, much of its vital "look" will have disappeared. You want that fish to "swim" along your wall with the color and vitality it had in the water.

Get out your De-Liar and carefully weigh the fish, measure its length and greatest girth, and write down the figures in the notebook. That system is a lot better than committing the measurements to memory, which tends to wander in some of us older fellows, while others have been known to nudge the figures upward a mite.

All this ought to be done as quickly as possible so the fish can be put in a live-well or on a stringer while it is still lively. The goal is to keep it alive as long as possible if you're going to stay out on the lake or stream for a while.

It's generally not practical to take a fish directly to a taxidermist. Most of us want to take it home for show and tell. It's at this stage that the majority of the critical mistakes in trophy-fish care are made, according to Lannie Ballard of Ballard Taxidermy in Woodbridge, Virginia. Ballard knows whereof he speaks. Among his recent jobs was restoration work on the famous Chadwick ram mount, No. 1 Stone sheep in the Boone and Crockett Club record book.

Let's assume you've just come off the water and it's time to kill the fish. Catching it has given you one of your greatest outdoor experiences, and the fish—like any species of fish or game—deserves to be treated with respect. To kill it as quickly and humanely as possible, take the small knife and insert the fine, narrow blade into the head just behind the eye. Do this on the side of the fish opposite the side you photographed, and try not to let the knife penetrate the skin on the far side. This will dispatch the fish instantly and do minimal damage to the skin.

Do not cut the fish in any other way, Ballard advises. Don't gut it. A good taxidermist can repair a slit up the belly, but all of them prefer that the body integrity be maintained. If you simply must gut the fish, make a horizontal cut up above the belly, on the side that will go against the wall. Make it only as long as is necessary to remove the entrails.

The next step is to dampen the terrycloth towel and wrap the fish in it. Put the package in a large plastic bag, and get it on ice—either a freezer or in a chest. If it's in a chest and you face a long drive home, empty the water from the chest occasionally. The terrycloth holds water and provides protection, and using it is much preferred to simply sticking the fish in a plastic bag.

Modern fish mounts, Ballard told me, employ either the original skin itself or a fiberglass mold. Most large fish are prepared with molds that are standardized for the various species. Freshwater fish are easier to skin-mount, and that system permits a more accurate recreation.

Ballard warned against what he called "an attitude of fast-food taxidermy." A good fish-mounting job takes time, so if the taxidermist tells you he'll call in six to eight months, be patient enough to wait for the call. A reputable craftsman won't try to save time by taking shortcuts—like forced drying of the trophy. Forced drying can cause the skin to crack and may shorten the life of the mount.

And finally, do some research. Talk to friends, sporting-goods dealers, and others about local taxidermists who can be expected to do a good job. Ask to see examples of their work on fish, not game animals.

What should you expect to pay for a quality fish mount? In most parts of the country, $6 to $10 an inch is probably the average range. Be aware that you may be quoted a low price "per inch, length and girth." A pot-bellied largemouth bass can have a girth nearly equal to its length, so such a quote would probably be something less than a bargain.

Generally, it's best to shop around for quality work and be willing to pay a fair price for it, rather than seeking the least-expensive job you can get. "You get what you pay for" is a phrase that applies in spades to taxidermy. Seek out friends and acquaintances with fish mounts, and look those mounts over carefully. Is the fish's coloration accurate? Is its attitude one of action and "aliveness," or does it just hang there like, well, like a stuffed fish? Ask the owner's opinion of the craftsman who did the work.

All the field care and sleuthing will pay off when you pick up your trophy and place it in that special spot in your home. What you have now, up there for all to see, is a piece of artwork, an investment, but most important, the proof of an angler's dream come true.

My Favorite Quotes and Quips

I'm a word guy, and my office wall here at home is plastered with pithy quotes, sayings, poetry (some questionable), and inspiration that I've been collecting for half a century. As you might suspect, each is an eloquent expression of the natural world's beauty, values, and allure to those who wander there. Allow me to share some of my favorite "words out of time" with you. I've included the attribution for each when known:

"Rich," the Old Man said dreamily, "is not baying after what you can't have. Rich is having the time to do what you want to do. Rich is a little whiskey to drink and some food to eat and a roof over your head and a fish pole and a boat and a gun and a dollar for a box of shells. Rich is not owing any money to anybody, and not spending what you haven't got."
Robert Ruark, *The Old Man and the Boy*

"It takes a long time to become young."
Pablo Picasso

"Knowledge makes arrogant, but love edifies. If anyone supposes that he knows anything, he has not yet known as he ought to know."
1 Corinthians, 8: 1-2 (NAS)

"There's no sense in going further . . .

It's the edge of cultivation."
So they said, and I believed it . . . .
Till a voice, as bad as conscience,
Rang interminable changes
On one everlasting Whisper
Day and night repeated—so:

Something hidden.
Go and find it.
Go and look behind the Ranges . . .
Something lost behind the Ranges.
Lost and waiting for you.
GO!
Rudyard Kipling, *The Explorer*

"Life itself . . . is best when it resembles dry-fly fishing."
M. L. Montgomery, *The Way of the Trout*

"There are some who can live without wild things and some who cannot . . . . Like winds and sunsets, wild things were taken for granted until progress began to do away with them. Now we face the question of whether a still higher 'standard of living' is worth its costs in things natural, wild, and free. For us of the minority, the opportunity to see geese is more important than television, and the chance to find a pasque-flower is a right as inalienable as free speech."
Aldo Leopold, *A Sand County Almanac*

"I do not look upon wildlife as a sacred cow—as some nature lovers do—but as a wild product of the land that can and should be used sustainably as an integral part of mankind's life-support system."
Ron Thomson, *Shadrek*

"If you pursue happiness, it will elude you. But if you focus on your family, your friends, the needs of others, and doing the very best you can, happiness will find *you*."
Unknown

"Do not follow where the path may lead. Go instead where there is no path—and leave a trail."
Ralph Waldo Emerson

"What are we going to do if there be no more deer in the pines . . . no more snipe whistling in the meadows . . . no more piping of widgeon and chattering of teal? And when the dawn wind stirs through the ancient cottonwoods and the gray light steals down from the hills, what if there be no more goose music?"
Aldo Leopold, *A Sand County Almanac*

"Give a man a fish
And he eats for a day.
Teach a man to fish
And he sits in a boat
And drinks beer all day."
An Old Irish Proverb

"The hunter is the arch-type of freedom. His well-being rests in no man's hand but his own."
Theodore Roosevelt

"When despair grows in me
And I wake in the middle of the night at the least sound
In fear of what my life and my children's lives may be,
I go and lie down where the wood drake
Rests in his beauty on the water, and the great heron feeds.
I come into the peace of wild things
Who do not tax their lives with forethought of grief.
I come into the presence of still water.
And I feel above me the day-blind stars
Waiting for their light. For a time
I rest in the grace of the world, and am free."
Wendell Berry, *The Peace of Wild Things*

"Not all who wander are lost."
J. R. R. Tolkien, *The Lord of the Rings*

"Thus use your frog …. Put your hook through his mouth, and out at his gills; … and then with a fine needle and silk sew the upper part of his leg, with only one stitch, to the arming-wire of your hook; or tie the frog's leg, above the upper joint, to the armed-wire; and in so doing use him as though you loved him."

Izaak Walton, *The Compleat Angler*

"If there are no dogs in Heaven, then when I die I want to go where they went."
Will Rogers

"Lord, I believe, help now my unbelief—
The old cry echoes down the centuries.
We pray in doubt, mixing our joy with grief,
And mount our mountain slowly, on our knees.
We cannot see, and so we only grope
Across the maze our life seems fashioned of,
And reach and seek and think and feel—and hope
That when we find the truth, it will be Love."
James Dillet Freeman, *I Believe*

"What would the world be, once bereft
Of wet and wilderness? Let them be left
O let them be left, wilderness and wet;
Long live the weeds, and the wilderness yet."
Gerard Manley Hopkins

"Life is not a journey to the grave with the intention of arriving safely in a pretty and well-preserved body, but rather to skid in broadside, thoroughly used up, totally worn out, and loudly proclaiming…'Wow—what a ride!'"
Unknown

"…he that hopes to be a good angler must not only bring an inquiring, searching, observing wit, but he must bring a large measure of hope and patience, and a love and propensity to the art itself; but having

once got and practiced it, then doubt not but angling will prove to be
so pleasant that it will be, like virtue, a reward to itself.
Izaak Walton

The Fisherman's Favorite Bait

This is the bait the fishermen take,
The fishermen take, the fishermen take,
When they start out the fish to wake
So early in the morning.

They take a nip before they go—
A good one, ah! And long and slow
So early in the morning.

Another when they're on the street
Which they repeat each time they meet
For "luck"—for that's the way they greet
A fisher in the morning.

And when they are on the river's brink,
Again they drink without a wink
To fight malaria—all by the doctor's warning.

They tip a flask with true delight
When there's a bite; if fishing's light,
They smile the more till jolly tight,
All fishing they are scorning.

Another nip as they depart;
One at the mart and one to part,
But none when in the house they dart,
Expecting there'll be mourning.

This is the bait the fishermen try
Who fishes buy at prices high,
And tell each one a bigger lie
Of fishing in the morning.
Unknown

Images of a Trail Ride

Savor with me the reflections of a dude in paradise...

There are very few moments in my life that won't fade with time. I'm pretty sure my mind's eye will never completely lose the picture imprinted on it one brilliant July morning. Our string of saddlehorses emerged from heavy timber onto the shore of an incredibly clear blue-green lake nestled on the floor of a magnificent circular glacial basin. Rock walls towered more than a thousand feet heavenward, and white ribbons cascaded down the sheer faces from permanent snow fields. Trout seen from the high banks seemed to be finning slowly along through shimmering air.

Among the words that come to mind are awesome, spectacular, humbling. But no words can do justice to that place. The photos we took are almost insults. It's the most beautiful spot I've ever visited.

Seventeen of us had gathered a few days earlier at the Bob Marshall Wilderness Ranch in Seeley Lake, Montana, for one of the forty-odd Trail Riders of the Wilderness trips sponsored each year by the American Forestry Association. I was along as AFA representative and also because, as editor of its *American Forests* magazine, I needed to learn first-hand about the Trail Riders program.

I had a lot of learning to do. The word "dude" was invented to describe people like me. I'd spent a lot of time in wild country and had even flown a fair amount of hours in bush planes, but only three times previously had my personality been plunked against a saddle. And here we were about to embark on 150 miles or so on horseback. Thankfully, many other members of our congenial group were in the same boat. So when I boarded old Banner, a sure-footed palomino, on the first sun-gilded morning of our ten-day odyssey, there were no worries about sore muscles—only an irrepressible excitement about what was to come.

Often a long-awaited vacation doesn't quite measure up to the pretrip anticipation and plan-making. But all the daydreams and night dreams I had before heading for western Montana were far surpassed by the matchless experiences of those ten days. The post-trip daydreams are much better. I have them often. Share a few of them now with me.

VISTAS: Lord, how beautiful the Rockies are! All my life I'd wanted to come here, and I've finally made it. On our first day out, the string winds high into the Swan Mountains. At one spot, a rider can look down and see, about six inches to the right of his horse's hooves but hundreds of feet below, the tops of big ponderosa pines, looking like furry needles. But who can look downward when the view outward is so compelling? Across the vast Swan River valley is the snow-streaked Mission Range, reflected in the sparkling surface of deep, clear Holland Lake. I scramble up the steep slope to capture the scene on film, trying to avoid impaling myself on those furry needles far below.

Some days later we dismount above timberline and clamber up through a meadow carpeted with wildflowers to an outcropping atop Haystack Mountain. We can only stand speechless and drink in an awesome sweep of peaks, tier upon tier, some with snow spots, as far as the eye can see in every direction—a place of monumental immensity and grandeur. Dominating it is the Chinese Wall, an escarpment plummeting a thousand feet straight down and extending lengthwise some twelve miles. A world of eagles and mountain goats, and very graced humans who do not stay but who come away renewed and enriched and humbled and uplifted.

Where there is splendor, there is God.

CAMP SCENES: A see-your-breath morning along Feline Creek. The stoked-up sheepherder stove broadcasts an invitation to a breakfast of bacon and trout and homefries. A sharp-eyed wrangler spots five white mountain goats feeding along a green slope far above us. I gawk at them so long through binoculars that my neck hurts half that day.

Not so far up the slope is a sizable patch of old snow. A few of us can't resist the temptation of a snowball fight, and we scramble up and fire away. Direct hits are few—we don't know each other well enough yet. But the feel of snow in July—grains of the old snowbank sticking to our hands—is an exhilarating sensation that Dick Leppo,

Lynda Koch, Maggie Gausewitz, and others of us share. Our meandering route back to camp is dotted with diminutive red and white
and yellow and purple wildflowers.

**Morning in a mountain meadow camp. Cutthroat trout
will bend this rod today.**

At Murphy Flats, our next stopover, our red-and-blue two-person
tents delineate the curvature of the bank of the South Fork of the
Flathead River. Stove smoke rises from a copse of pines. At day's
end after a hard ride, the saddle horses and pack mules—released
one by one from their human burdens and the restraining bridles and
saddles—race out into the open flat to graze and roll gloriously in
the dust, freedom flaunted by every rippling muscle and flying mane.

The "rodeo" over, we gather near one of the tents for evening
sundowners. There's easy talk, and laughter, and a quiet reveling in
the parts of the day that were special to each of us. We are strangers
no more. Maggie, our expert on things natural, pulls from her duffel
diagrams of the constellations in the northern sky. We lay back, arms
cushioning heads, and listen to the soft words; the night sky begins
to pulse with life: the Hunter, the Bear, the Dragon ....

Another campsite on the upper South Fork: late sun slants
through lacy branches ... Cathedral in the Pines. A Frisbee game

150

makes happy noise in a mountain meadow. A Canada jay joins us for dinner, earning his nickname of camp-robber. At just about full dark, a mule-deer doe meanders through the Frisbee field, and shortly thereafter, other shapes move slowly into camp. It's young wrangler Dave Toelke, returning on horseback with three well-loaded mules after a sixty-five-mile round trip to bring in fresh grub.

Our final camp is in deep forest on a mountain bench. Firelight flickers on pensive faces. Tomorrow it's paradise lost. Someone starts a song, and other voices blend in. Somehow tomorrow fades and the surrounding blackness softens.

FISHING: It's been said in certain quarters that when it comes to fishing, I stand anywhere from fanatic to paranoid. That's absolutely true. And the Bob Marshall Wilderness has just about tipped me over the edge.

I spend our first layover day fishing the Flathead River. Its bed and banks are littered with round, white boulders, and getting around is like trying to walk on greased bowling balls. In this area the river is a series of bright blue veins, separated by islets of green spruce and pine, flowing spiritedly through a wild valley. I'm so fired up by the sight of fish dimpling the surface that my shaking hands can't handle the simple task of knotting leader to fly.

The trout fishing is unquestionably the finest I've ever had anywhere. On this unforgettable day, I catch at least fifty trout up to sixteen inches long, all on dry flies. They are cutthroat trout—beautiful, sleek fish so named for the crimson slash on the undersides of the gills. The belly is a brush-stroke of blood-red. I release all but five, which will grease up the big frypan the next morning.

Somewhere in the middle of that idyllic day, I take it all off and engage in what can be called either skinnydipping or a *very* quick bath. Though it's July, the water is still partly made up of snowmelt. The self-timer on my camera enables me to capture for posterity (or something) a shot of an editor, naked as a jaybird and about as blue as the sky, emerging double-time from a pool on the river.

Another day, I hike a mile down a mountain trail to gorgeous little Gordon Creek—sun-flecked riffles, emerald pools. At one spot the stream narrows to about eight feet and flows past a sheer rock ledge, the lips of which slant down into deep water: a perfect lair for a trout. I cast a Grizzly Bivisible dry fly so that it alights above that spot and drifts jauntily over it. He is there—I see him knifing up through the depths. He takes the fly and continues up and out of the water, his fifteen-inch length clearing the surface by at least a foot, suspended at the top of his arc in a magic instant, his red cutthroat jaw a laser spot of color against the enveloping forest green.

ON THE TRAIL: Dudes learn pretty quickly that they can entrust their lives to their horses. Dizzying slopes, boulder-strewn riverbeds, rocky drop-offs in deep forest—all are as city sidewalks to these amazing animals.

It can be disconcerting to see your mount grab a mouthful of trailside salad while negotiating a forty-five-degree pitch, or to have him suddenly leap across a blowdown tree along the trail (followed immediately by considerable snickering from Blanche Houseknecht, the gal in the black cowboy hat on the horse behind).

And along about the third day, I have misgivings about whether I'll ever learn to match my rhythm with that of my friend Banner. He seems always to be going up when I'm coming down. But as the miles melt by, the contact of horse and human rump becomes a familiar, friendly feeling, like the fit of well-broken-in moccasins, a feeling garnished by the knowledge that this enigmatic animal is taking me along thread-thin trails to an experience of a lifetime.

One azure day we are riding single-file through a small forest patch on Murphy Flats. A hand goes up at the head of the string, and the word filters back—cougar! Only the wrangler at the head sees the big cat, which had been coming toward us along the trail, but we all see the fresh hand-size prints in the dust.

There is something elemental in that moment for me, something about age-old instincts and man's connection with wild country, something I'm fearful my children may not be able to experience. The sight of bear droppings later on brings the same sensation.

LITTLE THINGS:

Sounds: Horse bells to wake up by; a burbling creek to nod off with. The swishing of horses' tails. Low murmur of our group at dinner. The soughing of a mountain breeze in ponderosa pines.

*Smells:*The wonderful scents of pine and spruce and lacy larch. Trail dust. Breakfast trout. Leather and horses.

Feels: The warmth of a coffee cup in the mountain night. Oily tack. The balance of a good flyrod.

PEOPLE: I've saved the best for last. A Trail Ride is a very personal experience. Each of us savored different things, assessed the sweep of the days against a different set of values and ground rules. But it was the sharing of those individual experiences that enriched them, gave them far more meaning than they could possibly have had if enjoyed alone and kept to oneself.

Our trip was in every respect an experience of people, a communion of spirits. Each of us brought something to the others. Let me introduce you ....

Sister Suzy Bartuss and Sister Jodie Guisinger, two once-cloistered nuns who now devote their lives to praying for and supporting people in need. Quick to laugh, easily accepting others, and endearing themselves to all by their friendliness and their doting care of their horses. Sister Jodie's unexpected dunking in a creek one chilly morning brought a wide-eyed *"Oooh, is that cold!"*

Tom Buckley and Blanche Houseknecht, a boisterous, gravelly voiced Irishman and his attractive freckle-faced wife from Noo Yawk. Each of them caught a nice trout, and they're still "discussing" whose was bigger.

Chris Collinsworth and Pat Baron, two young teachers from Michigan—Pat the Frisbee champ, Chris the budding fisherperson. These two put up a tent but never used it, preferring to sleep out under the star-glistening Montana big sky. Count on them to be last in the breakfast line.

Mary Corddry, reporter for the *Baltimore Sun* newspapers. We could always spot Mary on the trail; she was the one directly beneath a furry, floppy, light tan trail hat perched at a jaunty angle. Both hat and wearer are one of a kind.

Mary Hoffman, a chemist from Ohio and an experienced rider and hiker. Quiet, helpful to genuine dude types.

Dick and Thel Leppo, an Ohio businessman and his corporate secretary (who's also his wife). Hosts for the "sundowner circle." Usually arm in arm at day's end. Dick's first-ever beard drew mixed reviews.

Maggie Gausewitz, medical technician from Missouri. Maggie is very likely AFA's champion Trail Rider. This was her twenty-eighth ride. A joy to be with and a true observer of nature, who admits she can't seem to outgrow her enthusiasm for the mountains.

Lynda Koch, living proof that there is a town called Ypsilanti, Michigan. She was a Frisbee flunkout, and her aim with a snowball was abominable. But her enthusiasm for riding and just about everything else was catching.

Frank Hensley, a Chicago art director, flipped a coin with Herb Ochsner to see who would wind up with me as a tentmate. Frank lost. Frank's a fine rider, recognizable by his Tom Mix hat. He and I hiked around that glacial lake, catching trout and gazing at the grandeur.

Herb Ochsner, a career Forest Service employee, now retired and living in North Carolina. He won the coin toss and had a tent to himself. Just as well—he snores. Amazingly agile for his seventy-two years, as witness a long hike up the Chinese Wall.

Bob and Dorothy Manchester, the trip doctor and his attractive wife, from Arizona. Doc had few medical demands, so he could concentrate on fishing and riding tall in the saddle.

The people mainly responsible for the success of our trip, and the catalysts for our coming together in spirit, were Virgil and Barbara Burns, our outfitters and the proprietors of the Bob Marshall Wilderness Ranch. The trip's practical arrangements—selection and care of campsites, healthy animals, food, and all the rest—were outstanding. (Incidentally, a sheepherder stove is a woodburner that consists of nothing more than two rectangular sheet-metal boxes and a smoke pipe. You wouldn't believe what red-haired Barbara can create on that contraption—turkey, roasts, pies, cakes, and plenty of them.)

But the Burnses did more than just *do* for us. These are tough, durable people who are able to meet this up-and-down country on its own terms. They are also good people who care about each other and their kids and their dudes. It was partly because of those qualities that at trip's end, as twenty-three of us lay around the ranch yard, there were no "guests" or "crew"—just people enjoying each other's company. I've never been anyplace where people worked so hard to please paying guests and at the same time made them feel so much like friends.

My hat's off to Virgil and Barbara, and to their able crew: Cheryll Moran, Larry Strange, Dave Toelke, and Harley Hettick.

ONE FINAL IMAGE: It is evening of a warm day, and I stand alone in the still valley of the Flathead, the river foaming at my feet. A storm forms on the far side of the valley. The low sun behind me illuminates the top half of the mountains beyond me, turning the trees to green flame. Against the backdrop of black thunderhead clouds, a double rainbow materializes, seeming to rise out of the green brilliance of the mountaintop, in a scene of indescribable beauty. Even the fishing is forgotten as I thank and praise the Father of us all for the gift of that moment.

My Shadows

Dear Spouse and I have lived in this area of central Virginia for two years now, but we're still discovering some of the little pleasures Rockbridge County serves up to us "outsiders"—people with a tendency to spend a lot of time beyond the confines of their nice warm homes. Yes, autumn still holds sway as this is written, but if you stuck your nose out the door this morning, it would be red and runny when you pulled it back in. Even in winter, little delights await out there. All that's required is awareness and a receptive attitude.

'Course, it helps if you're retired, as I am, but retired isn't required for a hike of moderate distance on a fine morning. I do that most mornings right from my back door, accompanied by Shadow No. 1—Sam, our enthusiastic but aging yellow Labrador, whom you've met before if you've read many of my previous rantings.

Sam is a companion par excellence—the finest nonhuman creature in all the civilized world. He roams at will on and off our local road, terrorizing such neighborhood nasties as moles, chipmunks, the especially hated squirrels, and the odd snake and groundhog.

And on one memorable morning ramble, Sam began barking at something in the high weeds along our road. Immediately suspecting a disaster in the making, I ran to him and tried to get him away from the object of his ire. But I was too late: It was a skunk, and just as I lunged for the dog, he lunged for the white-striped rodent. In an instant Sam recognized the error of his ways, backing up and slobbering and rubbing his prominent proboscis.

I pulled him farther away and went as close as I dared to the skunk, which was a whole lot more frightened than either of us was, and could see that it was only about two-thirds grown. I thanked the Big Guy that the animal's scent gland was not fully developed and Sam had suffered only a "glancing blow." But he was *persona non grata* in the house for a few days.

Sam treats our larger neighbors, the sloe-eyed and graceful (not to mention delicious) *Odocoileus virginianus*, or whitetailed deer, with more respect and deference. Believe it or not, when one of them crosses the road, he will obey my command to sit, and will watch the animal with me for maybe fifteen seconds. When he can't stand it anymore, he'll "break point" and give chase, but quickly gives it up as a lost cause.

Among the other delights of a walk of a mile or two at sunup are the feathered characters you're likely to encounter. I find two of them especially captivating: One is the redtailed hawk. A pair live in the forested sinkhole behind our house, and the two became four earlier this year (the young—or maybe the old folks, who knows?—have since moved on to less crowded skies). A couple of tall, dead trees, their branches starkly skeletal against the morning sky, are among the favorite perches for "our" redtails. It's a treat to watch them soar and wheel, the low sun illuminating the rusty-red tail feathers that reveal their species.

My other revered bird is the pileated woodpecker (*Dryocopus pileatus*), largest woodpecker in North America, with adults reaching an overall length of nineteen inches. Mostly black with a red crest and a white line down the sides of the throat, its wings flash white during its up-and-down trips from tree to tree as it searches for juicy insects. This bird's drumming can be incredibly loud, as if someone were whacking the tree with a hammer. Its call is distinctive, best described as a wild laugh. Watching a pair of these crow-size characters working a woodlot is a real hoot.

Let's see: What have I forgotten? Oh, yes, the title does mention shadows. My other shadow companion on my morning walks, in addition to the big yellow one, is, well, me. Sections of the local road run along fescue fields that slope down sharply to the west. On those delightful clear mornings when I happen to be afield just as the early sun is topping the spine of the Blue Ridge to the east, my "other" shadow mimics my every step. When the sun's rays are at their sharpest angle, I'm walking not only on the road but also as far as 200 yards away, down in the fields. As the sun gets higher in the sky, the other me moves uphill and gets more companionable. It's a neat sensation that seldom fails to bring a smile.

I highly recommend a morning ramble. It's good for the spirit.

Email to family, June 10, 2014

Hey, All, thought you might like to hear about my fishing trip yesterday and its highlights:

Went out about 9 a.m. with Ol' Sam to wade-fish the nearby Maury River. Just wore a T-shirt and shorts and wading shoes with well-worn felt soles and metal spikes to give some stability on the river's jillion round rocks. Caught some small fish, lost a pretty nice smallmouth bass. Slipped and went under. Ruined my cell phone, which I'd forgotten to put in a Ziplock bag. Fast water cleaned green snot off my handkerchief. Caught some more small fish.

Sun was mostly behind clouds, but I need my special sunglasses with a magnifier area at bottom to tie knots when I change lures. Standing in rapids, I fell in again and watched helpless as my new sunglasses slipped from my grasp and moved downstream into deep water twice as fast as I could follow.

After falling in a third time (and, of course, catching a few more inedible small fish), I was tying on my favorite lure, the Crickhopper, when it slipped from my grasp and headed downstream. By this time I was beyond worrying about falling in again, so I lurched forward and managed to grasp the little lure. Unfortunately, it was still tied to the line and for some arcane reason I yanked on the line and the lure's front treble hook (very small, fine hooks) sank into my left thumb beyond the barb, and the rear treble hook plowed into my middle finger—yes, beyond the barb. The two fingers were clamped about a quarter-inch apart and so the hooks were nearly inaccessible. Couldn't grab hooks with fingers of other hand, so eventually I used the hook on another lure (a jig, in case you're interested) to yank the barbs out. Pain was modest, and the blood should have cleared out of the river by now. Sam appeared to be laughing at me.

Deciding I'd had enough fun for one day, I walked the mile and a half to the car and headed home, where I poured a glass of Irish sippin' whiskey. Life is good!

I've saved the story below for last. Its author, Corey Ford, was one of a handful of outdoor writers of the middle to late 1900s— along with the likes of Robert Ruark, Gene Hill, and Charlie Elliott— whose words literally seduced me as I was growing up. His classics include "The Lower Forty," a series of delightful columns that ran in Field & Stream. *But his finest creation—and to my mind a strong candidate for the best outdoor story ever written—is "The Road to Tinkhamtown," published for the first time in* Field & Stream *in 1970, after his death.*

Though it is fiction, it evokes the elemental relationship between the natural world and those who are drawn to it. If you have not read this piece, and especially if you have more than a few years behind you, it will touch you to the core.

The Road to Tinkhamtown
By Corey Ford

It was a long way, but he knew where he was going. He would follow the road through the woods and over the crest of a hill and down the hill to the stream, and cross the sagging timbers of the bridge, and on the other side would be the place called Tinkhamtown. He was going back to Tinkhamtown.

He walked slowly at first, his legs dragging with each step. He had not walked for almost a year, and his flanks had shriveled and wasted away from lying in bed so long; he could fit his fingers around his thigh. Doc Towle had said he would never walk again, but that was Doc for you, always on the pessimistic side. Why, now he was walking quite easily, once he had started. The strength was coming back into his legs, and he did not have to stop for breath so often. He tried jogging a few steps, just to show he could, but he slowed again because he had a long way to go.

It was hard to make out the old road, choked with alders and covered by matted leaves, and he shut his eyes so he could see it better. He could always see it when he shut his eyes. Yes, here was the beaver dam on the right, just as he remembered it, and the flooded stretch where he had picked his way from hummock to hummock while the dog splashed unconcernedly in front of him. The water had been over his boot tops in one place, and sure enough, as he waded it now his left boot filled with water again, the same warm squdgy feeling. Everything was the way it had been that afternoon—nothing had changed in ten years. Here was the blowdown across the road that he had clambered over, and here on a knoll was the clump of thornapples where a grouse had flushed as they passed. Shad had wanted to look for it, but he had whistled him back. They were looking for Tinkhamtown.

He had come across the name on a map in the town library. He used to study the old maps and survey charts of the state; sometimes they showed where a farming community had flourished a century ago, and around the abandoned pastures and in the orchards grown up in pine the birds would be feeding undisturbed. Some of his best grouse covers had been located that way. The map had been rolled up in a cardboard cylinder; it crackled with age as he spread it out. The map was dated 1857. It was the sector between Cardigan and Kearsarge Mountains, a wasteland of slash and second-growth timber without habitation today, but evidently it had supported a number of families before the Civil War. A road was marked on the map, dotted with Xs for homesteads, and the names of the owners were lettered beside them: Nason, J. Tinkham, Allard, R. Tinkham. Half the names were Tinkham. In the center of the map—the paper was so yellow that he could barely make it out—was the word "Tinkhamtown."

He had drawn a rough sketch on the back of an envelope, noting where the road left the highway and ran north to a fork and then turned east and crossed a stream that was not even named; and the next morning he and Shad had set out together to find the place. They could not drive very far in the Jeep because washouts had gutted the roadbed and laid bare the ledges and boulders. He had stuffed the sketch in his hunting-coat pocket, and hung his shotgun over his forearm and started walking, the setter trotting ahead with the bell on his collar tinkling. It was an old-fashioned sleighbell, and it had a thin, silvery note that echoed through the woods like peepers in the spring. He could follow the sound in the thickest cover, and when it stopped he would go to where he'd heard it last and Shad would be on point. After Shad's death, he had put the bell away. He'd never had another dog.

It was silent in the woods without the bell, and the way was longer than he remembered. He should have come to the big hill by now. Maybe he'd taken the wrong turn back at the fork. He thrust a hand into his hunting coat; the envelope with the sketch was still in the pocket. He sat down on a flat rock to get his bearings, and then he realized, with a surge of excitement, that he had stopped on this very rock for lunch ten years ago. Here was the waxed paper from his sandwich, tucked in a crevice, and here was the hollow in the leaves where Shad had stretched out beside him, the dog's soft muzzle flattened on his thigh. He looked up, and through the trees he could see the hill.

He rose and started walking again, carrying his shotgun. He had left the gun standing in its rack in the kitchen when he had been taken to the state hospital, but now it was hooked over his arm by the trigger guard; he could feel the solid heft of it. The woods grew more dense as he climbed, but here and there a shaft of sunlight slanted through the trees. *And there were forests ancient as the hills,* he thought, *enfolding sunny spots of greenery.* Funny that should come back to him now; he hadn't read it since he was a boy. Other things were coming back to him—the smell of dank leaves and sweetfern and frosted apples, the sharp contrast of sun and cool shade, the

November stillness before snow. He walked faster, feeling the excitement swell within him.

He paused on the crest of the hill, straining his ears for the faint mutter of the stream below him, but he could not hear it because of the voices. He wished they would stop talking so he could hear the stream. Someone was saying his name over and over, "Frank, Frank," and he opened his eyes reluctantly and looked up at his sister. Her face was worried, and there was nothing to worry about. He tried to tell her where he was going, but when he moved his lips the words would not form. "What did you say, Frank?" she asked, bending her head lower. "I don't understand." He couldn't make the words any clearer, and she straightened and said to Doc Towle: "It sounded like Tinkhamtown."

"Tinkhamtown?" Doc shook his head. "Never heard him mention any place by that name."

He smiled to himself. Of course he'd never mentioned it to Doc. Things like a secret grouse cover you didn't mention to anyone, not even to as close a friend as Doc was. No, he and Shad were the only ones who knew. They had found it together, that long-ago afternoon, and it was their secret.

They had come to the stream—he shut his eyes so he could see it again—and Shad had trotted across the bridge. He had followed more cautiously, avoiding the loose planks and walking along a beam with his shotgun held out to balance himself. On the other side of the stream the road mounted steeply to a clearing in the woods, and he halted before the split-stone foundations of a house, the first of the series of farms shown on the map. It must have been a long time since the building had fallen in; the cottonwoods growing in the cellar hole were twenty, maybe thirty years old. His boot overturned a rusted ax blade and the handle of a china cup in the grass; that was all. Beside the doorstep was a lilac bush, almost as tall as the cottonwoods. He thought of the wife who had set it out, a little shrub then, and the husband who had chided her for wasting time on such frivolous things with all the farm work to be done. But the work had come to nothing, and still the lilac bloomed each spring, the one thing that had survived.

Shad's bell was moving along the stone wall at the edge of the clearing, and he strolled after the dog, not hunting, wondering about the people who had gone away and left their walls to crumble and their buildings to collapse under the winter snows. Had they ever come back to Tinkhamtown? Were they here now, watching him unseen? His toe stubbed against a block of hewn granite hidden by briars, part of the sill of the old barn. Once it had been a tight barn, warm with cattle steaming in their stalls, rich with the blend of hay and manure and harness leather. He liked to think of it the way it was; it was more real than this bare rectangle of blocks and the emptiness inside. He'd always felt that way about the past. Doc used to argue that what's over is over, but he would insist Doc was wrong. Everything is the way it was, he'd tell Doc. The past never changes. You leave it and go on to the present, but it is still there, waiting for you to come back to it.

He had been so wrapped in his thoughts that he had not realized Shad's bell had stopped. He hurried across the clearing, holding his gun ready. In a corner of the stone wall an ancient apple tree had littered the ground with fallen fruit, and beneath it Shad was standing motionless. The white fan of his tail was lifted a little and his backline was level, the neck craned forward, one foreleg cocked. His flanks were trembling with the nearness of grouse, and a thin skein of drool hung from his jowls. The dog did not move as he approached, but the brown eyes rolled back until their whites showed, looking for him. "Steady, boy," he called. His throat was tight, the way it always got when Shad was on point, and he had to swallow hard. "Steady, I'm coming."

"I think his lips moved just now," his sister's voice said. He did not open his eyes, because he was waiting for the grouse to get up in front of Shad, but he knew Doc Towle was looking at him. "He's sleeping," Doc said after a moment. "Maybe you better get some sleep yourself, Mrs. Duncombe." He heard Doc's heavy footsteps cross the room. "Call me if there's any change," Doc said as he closed the door, and in the silence he could hear his sister's chair creaking beside him, her silk dress rustling regularly as she breathed.

What was she doing here, he wondered. Why had she come all the way from California to see him? It was the first time they had seen each other since she had married and moved out West. She was his only relative, but they had never been very close; they had nothing in common, really. He heard from her now and then, but it was always the same letter: Why didn't he sell the old place—it was too big for him now that the folks had passed on—and take a small apartment in town where he wouldn't be alone? But he liked the big house, and he wasn't alone, not with Shad. He had closed off all the other rooms and moved into the kitchen so everything would be handy. His sister didn't approve of his bachelor ways, but it was very comfortable with his cot by the stove and Shad curled on the floor near him at night, whinnying and scratching the linoleum with his claws as he chased a bird in a dream. He wasn't alone when he heard that.

He had never married. He had looked after the folks as long as they lived; maybe that was why. Shad was his family. They were always together—Shad was short for Shadow—and there was a closeness between them that he did not feel for anyone else, not his sister or Doc even. He and Shad used to talk without words, each knowing what the other was thinking, and they could always find one another in the woods. He still remembered the little things about him: the possessive thrust of his paw, the way he false-yawned when he was vexed, the setter stubbornness sometimes, the clownish grin when they were going hunting, the kind eyes. That was it; Shad was the kindest person he had ever known.

They had not hunted again after Tinkhamtown. The old dog had stumbled several times walking back to the Jeep, and he had to carry him in his arms the last hundred yards. It was hard to realize he was gone. He liked to think of him the way he was; it was like the barn—more real than the emptiness. Sometimes at night, lying awake with the pain in his legs, he would hear the scratch of claws on the linoleum, and he would turn on the light and the hospital room would be empty. But when he turned the light off he would hear the scratching again, and he would be content and drop off to sleep, or what passed for sleep in these days and nights that ran together without dusk or dawn.

Once he asked Doc point-blank if he would ever get well. Doc was giving him something for the pain, and he hesitated a moment and finished what he was doing and cleaned the needle and then looked at him and said: "I'm afraid not, Frank." They had grown up in town together, and Doc knew him too well to lie. "I'm afraid there's nothing to do." Nothing to do but lie here and wait till it was over.

"Tell me, Doc," he whispered, for his voice wasn't very strong, "what happens when it's over?" And Doc fumbled with the catch of his black bag and closed it and said well he supposed you went on to someplace else called the Hereafter. But he shook his head; he always argued with Doc and now was no different: "No, it isn't someplace else," he told him. "It's someplace you've been where you want to be again." Doc didn't understand, and he couldn't explain it any better. He knew what he meant, but the shot was taking effect and he was tired.

He was tired now, and his legs ached a little as he started down the hill, trying to find the stream. It was too dark under the trees to see the sketch he had drawn, and he could not tell direction by the moss on the north side of the trunks. The moss grew all around the trees, swelling them out of size, and huge blowdowns blocked his way. Their upended roots were black and misshapen, and now instead of excitement he felt a surge of panic. He floundered through a pile of slash, his legs throbbing with pain as the sharp points stabbed him, but he did not have the strength to get to the other side and he had to back out again and circle. He did not know where he was going. It was getting late, and he had lost the way.

There was no sound in the woods, nothing to guide him, nothing but his sister's chair creaking and her breath catching now and then in a dry sob. She wanted him to turn back, and Doc wanted him to— they all wanted him to turn back. He thought of the big house; if he left it alone it would fall in with the winter snows and cottonwoods would grow in the cellar hole. And there were all the other doubts, but most of all there was the fear. He was afraid of the darkness, and being alone, and not knowing where he was going. It would be better to turn around and go back. He knew the way back.

And then he heard it, echoing through the woods like peepers in the spring, the thin, silvery tinkle of a sleighbell. He started running toward it, following the sound down the hill. His legs were strong again, and he hurdled the blowdowns, he leapt over fallen logs, he put one fingertip on a pile of slash and sailed over it like a grouse skimming. He was getting nearer and the sound filled his ears, louder than a thousand churchbells ringing, louder than all the choirs in the sky, as loud as the pounding of his heart. The fear was gone; he was not lost. He had the bell to guide him now.

He came to the stream, and paused for a moment at the bridge. He wanted to tell them he was happy — if they only knew how happy he was — but when he opened his eyes he could not see them anymore. Everything else was bright, but the room was dark.

The bell had stopped, and he looked across the stream. The other side was bathed in sunshine, and he could see the road mounting steeply, and the clearing in the woods, and the apple tree in a corner of the stone wall. Shad was standing motionless beneath it, the white fan of his tail lifted, his neck craned forward and one foreleg cocked. The whites of his eyes showed as he looked back, waiting for him.

"Steady," he called, "steady, boy." He started across the bridge. "I'm coming."

"The Road to Tinkhamtown" by Corey Ford is © Trustees of Dartmouth College. Reprinted by permission.

Final Words

So . . . is fishing love? I'm not sure. But I am convinced that fishing is, at the very least, a most pleasurable path that can lead to the One who knows the answer—because He is Perfect Love. What we seek, we fishermen—we humans—is not mere food. And it's not beneath the water. Thanks, Dad.

PESCADOR DE HOMBRES/LORD, YOU HAVE COME

Permission to reproduce this hymn, "Pescador de Hombres," has been granted by LicenSing Online.

CPSIA information can be obtained
at www.ICGtesting.com
Printed in the USA
LVOW01s1511090217
523694LV00013B/324/P